W9-BXX-128

Praise for
No Holds Barred

"This inspiring book is an invitation to bold, honest, and passionate communication with God. Mark Roberts points us to a biblical view of prayer, full of reality and reverence. Mark reminds us of the astounding freedom in prayer we find throughout the Psalms and encourages us to take advantage of that freedom. Read this book and discover your 'inner psalmist'!"

—MATT REDMAN, songwriter, worship leader, author of *Facedown*
and *The Unquenchable Worshipper*

"*No Holds Barred* is fresh, practical, and profound—a rarity in contemporary books on prayer. Mark Roberts gently guides us into more sincere prayer, helping us overcome our inhibitions and press into the bold and often shocking prayers of the Psalms. This book will richly reward those who take its truth to heart and who apply the principles Mark Roberts so ably explores."

—GARY THOMAS, author of *Sacred Pathways* and *Sacred Marriage*

"If you're tired of hiding from God, *No Holds Barred* could be your route to spiritual honesty. One chapter after another explores the well-traveled tributaries of the Psalms, ancient conduits for navigating the wonders, chaos, and tragedies of life."

—SALLY MORGENTHALER, author of *Worship Evangelism;* founder
of Sacramentis.com and Digital Glass Productions

"*No Holds Barred* personalizes the Psalms for me and gives me lots of tools to communicate with God. Mark Roberts shows us not just the actions and words of praying the Psalms but also the right heart, attitude, and theology behind those actions and words. This book will help you pray through the tough situations of life and will show you how to be utterly honest with God, no matter how you feel."

—ANDY PARK, worship leader, songwriter, and author
of *To Know You More*

"Mark Roberts gives us not only the permission but also the biblical mandate of wrestling with God in prayer. He writes with no holds barred as he invites us to discover profound theological truths and to participate in the book's practical exercises. In doing so, he brings us boldly to God's throne of grace with confidence."

—LIBBY VINCENT, Presbyterian pastor and adjunct professor
at Fuller Theological Seminary

"In *No Holds Barred,* Mark Roberts brings the unique perspective of pastor and theologian to one of the most pressing concerns of the day: How shall we pray, and specifically, how do the Psalms tell us to pray? As with his previous books, Mark blends the easy accessibility of a sermon with the deep learning of a scholar-theologian to bring every reader closer to the heart of the Psalms and thus to the heart of God."

—HUGH HEWITT, best-selling author and radio host
of the nationally syndicated *Hugh Hewitt Show*

NO HOLDS
BARRED

To Betty!
For what you are doing
for Laity's future, THANKS!

Mark O Rohlf
Dec. 2008

ALSO BY MARK ROBERTS

Jesus Revealed
Dare to Be True

NO HOLDS BARRED

BARRED

Wrestling with God in Prayer

MARK D. ROBERTS

WATERBROOK
PRESS

NO HOLDS BARRED
PUBLISHED BY WATERBROOK PRESS
2375 Telstar Drive, Suite 160
Colorado Springs, Colorado 80920
A division of Random House, Inc.

All Scripture quotations, unless otherwise indicated, are taken from the *New Revised Standard Version of the Bible,* copyright © 1989 by the Division of Christian Education of the National Council of the Churches of Christ in the USA. Used by permission. All rights reserved. Scripture quotations marked (NIV) are taken from the *Holy Bible, New International Version*®. NIV® Copyright © 1973, 1978, 1984 by International Bible Society. Used by permission of Zondervan Publishing House. All rights reserved. Scripture quotations marked (NLT) are taken from the *Holy Bible, New Living Translation,* copyright © 1996. Used by permission of Tyndale House Publishers, Inc., Wheaton, Illinois 60189. All rights reserved. Scripture quotations marked (KJV) are taken from the *King James Version.*

Italics in Scripture quotations reflect the author's added emphasis.

The author has made every effort to ensure the truthfulness of the stories and anecdotes in this book. In a few instances, names and identifying details have been changed to protect the privacy of the persons involved.

ISBN 1-57856-705-X

Copyright © 2005 by Mark D. Roberts

Published in association with Yates & Yates, LLP, Attorneys and Counselors, Orange, California.

All rights reserved. No part of this book may be reproduced or transmitted in any form or by any means, electronic or mechanical, including photocopying and recording, or by any information storage and retrieval system, without permission in writing from the publisher.

WATERBROOK and its deer design logo are registered trademarks of WaterBrook Press, a division of Random House, Inc.

Library of Congress Cataloging-in-Publication Data
Roberts, Mark D.
  No holds barred : wrestling with God in prayer / Mark D. Roberts.—1st ed.
     p. cm.
  Includes bibliographical references.
  ISBN 1-57856-705-X
  1. Bible. O.T. Psalms—Devotional use. 2. Prayer—Biblical teaching. 3. Prayer—Christianity.
I. Title.
BS1430.54R63 2005
248.3'2—dc22   2004022131

Printed in the United States of America
2005—First Edition

10 9 8 7 6 5 4 3 2 1

To my wife, Linda,
my partner in life and faith.
Your love, support, and friendship mean the world to me.
I thank God for you!

CONTENTS

ACKNOWLEDGMENTS

As always, I want to thank those who have joined me in the labor of publishing this book: Ron Lee, my editor at WaterBrook Press; Don Pape, my publisher; Don's helpful staff at WaterBrook; and Sealy and Curtis Yates of Yates and Yates, LLP, my literary agents and consistent encouragers.

I am continually thankful for my beloved congregation at Irvine Presbyterian Church. I am especially grateful for my ministry colleagues, both staff members and elders, and for my faithful friends in the Pastor's Study. It's a privilege to join with all of these folk in the adventure of knowing God better as we read, pray, and study the Psalms.

I also want to acknowledge those who have helped me go deeper in prayer and in the use of the Psalms. These people—theologians, songwriters, friends—have been my partners in discovery. They include John Calvin, Don Williams, David Clemensen, Buddy Owens, Matt Redman, Andy Park, Isaac Watts, C. S. Lewis, Eugene Peterson, Dietrich Bonhoeffer, and Walter Brueggemann.

My other partners, the most important of all, are my family members. The pages of this book are filled with stories from our life together. Thank you, Linda, Nathan, and Kara, for your faith, hope, and love.

As a deer longs for flowing streams,
　　so my soul longs for you, O God.
My soul thirsts for God,
　　for the living God.
When shall I come and behold
　　the face of God?

　　—Psalm 42:1-2

I stretch out my hands to you;
　　my soul thirsts for you like a parched land.

　　—Psalm 143:6

If I take the wings of the morning
　　and settle at the farthest limits of the sea,
even there your hand shall lead me,
　　and your right hand shall hold me fast.

　　—Psalm 139:9-10

NO HOLDS BARRED

Start Enjoying Audacious Freedom with God

I t was finally time to start writing this book. I looked forward to the task with anticipation but also with exhaustion. I had just finished a demanding year at church, with extra time devoted to writing, teaching, and serving as the volunteer second-grade music instructor in my children's school. I was worn out physically, emotionally, and spiritually—hardly the best way to begin writing a book.

Sensing the parched condition of my soul, my wife, Linda, suggested that I take a few days off. I soon found myself miles away from civilization in the Sierra Nevada mountains. My sanctuary was Kings Canyon, a glaciated gorge filled with lupine meadows and ponderosa pine forests. Soon I was sitting alongside the South Fork of the Kings River, marveling at the sheer granite cliffs towering above me and the turbulent river at my feet. The rare combination of a heavy snowpack and unseasonably hot weather had turned the South Fork into a roaring torrent.

Finding a private spot, I began praying through the Psalms. Many times before, when my soul was parched, I had turned to these ancient, poetic words of spirituality with a yearning for God's presence.

While I was reading, movement on the other side of the river caught my attention. A deer was exploring the opposite shore. I figured she was thirsty and looking for a safe place to drink. Finally she found a small cove where the river flowed less ferociously, and she waded into the water, where she remained for several minutes. Periodically she lowered her head to take a deep drink.

As I watched the deer, I saw an image of my own soul. I, too, had come to the Kings River with an intense thirst. It's no surprise that the first lines of Psalm 42 came to mind:

> As a deer longs for flowing streams,
>   so my soul longs for you, O God.
> My souls thirsts for God,
>   for the living God.
> When shall I come and behold
>   the face of God? (verses 1-2)

I'm generally not one to see life's coincidences as signs from God, but as I watched this deer, I had to wonder. I was preparing to write a book on experiencing God in prayer, but I was spiritually parched. And only fifteen yards away, a thirsty deer was drinking from a flowing stream. In more than four decades of hiking and camping in the wilderness, I had never seen anything like this. Was God helping me get in touch with my own thirst for him?

A Matter of Thirst

I don't know whether the Lord sent the deer. But I do know that he used it to break through the dry crust that had hardened my heart—a layer of stress and fatigue that had built up over the past months. As I watched the deer, I felt a yearning for God in a way I had not been able to feel for months. Like that deer, I wanted more than just a sip of living water. I yearned to wade into the healing flow of God's presence. I longed to drink deeply from the refreshing water of grace. And then to drink again.

Have you ever been so parched that you felt as though you would die if you couldn't wade into God's healing presence? Have you wanted to chip the crust off your heart so you could drink deeply from God's grace? If so, we're in this together. I wrote this book for you.

It's possible to get stuck in spiritual dryness for so long that you hardly feel a thirst for God anymore. You feel he's been silent and distant and unresponsive, so you think about giving up on pursuing him. But the thirst never completely disappears. Even when we seem to have lost our desire for God, something within us aches for the only One who can meet the deepest need of our parched souls. So if you feel only a twinge of desire for God, I've written this book for you, too.

But maybe you're experiencing unprecedented intimacy with God. You've known spiritual thirst in the past, but these days you're flooded with God's presence. If this is you, it's a great place to be. But I doubt that even now you're feeling that you've had enough. The more we experience the Lord, the more we realize how utterly desirable he is, and therefore the more we desire him. No one can get enough of God. So if you're drinking consistently from the heavenly stream, this book is also for you. It will help you drink more deeply and savor more completely the water of life.

A STRANGE, SAD IRONY

Sometimes in our parched spiritual state we can become—dare I say it?—*bored* in our relationship with God. This is one of the strangest, saddest ironies of the Christian life.

Notice that I'm not saying we become bored with God. Boredom with the real God is impossible. But we can become bored with our *relationship* with God. The fault lies not with our divine Friend but with the limitations we place on our friendship. We turn our backs on risky intimacy with God, accepting instead the harmless substitute of civility. We reject the excitement of God's nearness by keeping him at arm's length. We avoid his embrace, choosing instead to communicate with God mainly so we can deliver our list of predictable prayer requests, forgetting that he is a "refiner's fire" who wants to purify and mold us for his purposes (see Malachi 3:2). We relate to the Lion of Judah as if he were a safe house cat.

No wonder we get bored. I imagine that God finds such a limited relationship less than stimulating as well. Insulting, perhaps; interesting, no.

Our adherence to boring civility toward God is a product of our limited understanding of God's character. The nineteenth-century philosopher Friedrich Nietzsche maintained, "Against boredom even gods struggle in vain."[1] But Nietzsche underestimated the God of Abraham, Isaac, and Jacob, the

God who became flesh in Jesus Christ. The real God seeks an unadulterated, unrestrained, and utterly "unboring" relationship with us. And though God could compel us to do whatever he desires, he does not force us into intimacy with him. Instead, the Lover of our souls woos us away from spiritual boredom into the breathtaking adventure of genuine relationship with him.

WRESTLING WITH ABANDON

Neither you nor I will quench our soul's thirst unless we decide to do one thing, and to do it without hesitation. We must drop our inhibitions when we approach God. He's even less interested in a boring relationship than we are. So let's agree right now to plunge into a risky, exciting, expansive relationship with God. He invites us to wade right into his presence, sharing our whole selves with no holds barred.

In English, the expression *no holds barred* means "without limits or restraints." It's often used to describe a frank conversation where both parties opt for bluntness over politeness. Such a dialogue is risky because listeners might hear things that make them uncomfortable and because each person lets down his or her guard. Both parties are vulnerable and unprotected. And, though we may not feel completely comfortable doing so, this is exactly how we need to converse with God.

Initially, the phrase *no holds barred* had nothing to do with conversation. It was a term used in wrestling to describe a match that isn't constrained by official rules. If you've ever seen a serious wrestling match, in the Olympics, for example, you know that many holds are prohibited. You won't see any strangleholds, unlike what you might observe in a "professional" wrestling free-for-all.

Our typical approach to God brings to mind Olympic wrestling, in which every move is governed by detailed rules. Our communication with God is cautious, controlled, disciplined, and relentlessly boring. Fearful that we'll do something wrong or that God won't accept our true selves, we tame our prayers to the point that we actually hide our selves from the Lord. We pray without energy, without passion, and without honesty. In other words, we pray without thirst. It's easy to see why even God might have trouble staying fully engaged in such a lifeless conversation. He wants us to come at him with everything we've got.

It may seem irreverent to suggest that our relationship with God should in any way resemble the reckless antics of pro wrestling. But think about the all-night wrestling match Jacob found himself in. He wrestled with a being who appeared to be a man—no holds barred. As the sun arose, the mysterious figure asked Jacob to cry uncle. But Jacob refused to release his hold until the man blessed him, which he ultimately did. Afterward Jacob described the wrestling match: "I have seen God face to face, and yet my life is preserved" (Genesis 32:30). Although he appeared to grapple with a man, in fact Jacob went to the mat with the Lord himself. He came away with his life and, indeed, with divine blessing.

That's the type of wrestling God blesses. That's the type of all-out, nothing-held-back conversation he wishes we'd engage in through prayer.

Have you ever hung on to the Lord for dear life, not letting go until he blessed you? Have you ever told him everything that's on your heart, even the anger and bitterness, or the thankfulness and rejoicing, or the loneliness and doubt? Have you ever laid your soul bare before God, even though doing such a thing violates most of the rules you've been taught regarding proper prayer? If so, you have already wrestled with the Almighty. You are well on your way to a more authentic and more intimate relationship with God.

If you have never done such a thing, it's time to turn your back on spiritual boredom. Let's climb into the ring and accept God's invitation to no-holds-barred prayer.

God's Invitation to Authentic Prayer

Does God *really* want us to pray with such recklessness? Is this just a hare-brained idea for a book, or is there a solid biblical foundation for going toe-to-toe with the Almighty?

No scriptural text presents God's offer more clearly than Hebrews 4:14-16:

Since, then, we have a great high priest who has passed through the heavens, Jesus, the Son of God, let us hold fast to our confession. For we do not have a high priest who is unable to sympathize with our weaknesses, but we have one who in every respect has been tested as we are, yet without sin. *Let us therefore approach the throne of grace with boldness,* so that we may receive mercy and find grace to help in time of need.

As our great high priest, Jesus opened up unprecedented access to God. Through him we can "approach the throne of grace with boldness." The Greek word translated as "boldness" means more than "confidence," as it sometimes is rendered. Literally, it means "full freedom of speech" or "complete frankness."[2] Thus, as Christians we come before God with audacious freedom to tell him whatever is on our minds and hearts.

Unfortunately, the New Testament doesn't contain a collection of prayers that model such a bold approach to God's throne. But God hasn't left us without guidance in this area. He's given us the amazing gift of the Psalms, which German theologian Dietrich Bonhoeffer called "the Prayer Book of the Bible."[3] For ages Christians have turned to the Psalms to learn how to pray. As sixteenth-century theologian John Calvin observed, "a better and more unerring rule for guiding us in this exercise [of calling upon God] cannot be found elsewhere than in the Psalms." In fact, Calvin continued, "whatever may serve to encourage us when we are about to pray to God, is taught us in this book."[4]

Although the psalm writers offered their prayers prior to the high priestly work of Christ, their daring before God teaches, encourages, and challenges us. If anything, we who approach God in Christ should exercise *even greater* boldness than the psalmists. So if David can shock us with his prayer—"Get up, Lord! Save me, my God!" (Psalm 3:7)[5]—then shouldn't we feel the same freedom? And consider another of David's prayers, one of great impatience: "I am sick at heart. How long, O LORD, until you restore me?" (Psalm 6:3, NLT). Then, just three verses later, David complained,

I am weary with my moaning;
    every night I flood my bed with tears;
    I drench my couch with my weeping. (Psalm 6:6-7)

The freedom of expression that we see in the early psalms isn't limited to desperate pleas for help, however. Psalm 8 celebrates God's awesomeness with abandon: "O LORD, our Sovereign, how majestic is your name in all the earth!" (verse 1). Psalm 9 continues the joyful celebration:

> I will give thanks to the LORD with my whole heart;
>> I will tell of all your wonderful deeds.
> I will be glad and exult in you;
>> I will sing praise to your name, O Most High. (verses 1-2)

Whether crying out in agony, complaining with bitterness, begging for deliverance, or praising with joy, the psalmists consistently accepted God's invitation to bold prayer. Whether desperate with need or bursting with thanks, they didn't hold anything back.

WHY DO WE HOLD BACK?

Why can't we pray with at least the same freedom expressed by the psalmists? If Scripture provides both a theological foundation for no-holds-barred prayer and plentiful examples in the Psalms, why do we prefer restrained, sanitized, inauthentic prayers?

There are many reasons. Most of us were taught to talk to God not with abandon but instead with respectful reticence. I grew up praying the classic prayer "Now I Lay Me Down to Sleep." Though this nightly discipline was beneficial to some degree, the content of my prayer didn't exactly expand the parameters of my relationship with God.

Although I was raised in a church of deeply committed Christians, I can't recall hearing a fellow believer utter a gut-wrenching cry for divine help until I was well into my twenties. Good Presbyterians just didn't pray like that. No wonder I found it natural to pull my punches in prayer. What I learned from my community of faith became my own habit. I addressed the Lord reservedly, as if he were a traffic cop about to give me a ticket. I was so afraid of being penalized that even in desperate moments, I sensed that some holds just had to be barred with God.

An incomplete or inaccurate image of God can also limit our prayers. If we envision God as an angry tyrant, we'll keep our distance from his throne rather than walk up to him with boldness. Or if we picture God exclusively as the Chief Justice of the heavenly supreme court, we'll be disinclined to beg him for mercy. Conversely, our communication with God will be limited if we picture him in overly sentimental and familiar images. If God is merely my Friend and faithful Sidekick, then I'll freely express my needs to him, but not my worship.

Perhaps the most common reason we hesitate to come boldly before God is our sin. Since God is sinless and we are sinful, we correctly sense that we can't stroll nonchalantly into his presence as if our transgression were merely a minor inconvenience. If God is truly "a consuming fire," then we ought to approach him "with reverence and awe" (Hebrews 12:28-29). If you give it any thought at all, you'll think twice before speaking freely in the presence of a God who can burn you to a crisp.

Overcoming Our Ignorance

There is one other major reason we hold back in our communication with God. It's our ignorance of the Psalms. If we really knew these divinely inspired prayers, we'd imitate their astounding freedom. But our unfamiliarity with the Psalms inhibits our relationship with God.

Most of us think we know the Psalms, but at best we're familiar with a few "greatest hits." We probably sing portions of the Psalms in our worship services. But our knowledge of the Psalms is limited to relatively few familiar and comfortable passages. And when you think about it, many of the texts we sing in worship are excerpts from gutsy psalms, but with the messy parts removed. Thus we tend to be most familiar with only bits and pieces of the Psalms, and the more "acceptable" bits and pieces at that. A few beloved psalms and a few lyrical excerpts hardly represent the breadth and depth of this inspired, refreshing collection.

If you're looking for a compelling reason to let the Psalms, even the gut-wrenching ones, shape your relationship with God, you need look no further than Jesus himself. In his moment of deepest anguish as he was suffering on the cross, Jesus prayed from two psalms: "My God, my God, why have you forsaken me" (Psalm 22:1; Mark 15:34) and "Father, into your hands I commend my spirit" (Luke 23:46; see also Psalm 31:5). If Jesus prayed the Psalms, surely we ought to imitate his example.

Over half a century ago, Dietrich Bonhoeffer underscored the promise of this practice. "Whenever the Psalter is abandoned," he wrote, "an incomparable treasure vanishes from the Christian church. With its recovery will come unsuspected power."[6] It's the power to revive both your own soul and the church of Jesus Christ.

If ignorance of the Psalms is holding you back in your relationship with God, there's a simple solution. Get to know the Psalms! Admittedly, you'll find some unexpected peculiarity there. As Bible translator Eugene Peterson says, "the Psalms are queer fish."[7]

CONFRONTING THE UNCOMFORTABLE

I first confronted the fishiness of the Psalms three years ago during my sabbatical from Irvine Presbyterian Church. I began my time off with lofty plans: to write a book, to spend more time with my family, and, most of all, to renew my relationship with the Lord. I exulted in the realization that I wouldn't attend a committee meeting for 126 days!

My strategy for spiritual renewal was simple. I would pray systematically through the Psalms, taking a psalm each day, reading it, meditating on it, and offering it to God in prayer. I'd let the psalm inspire my personal prayers and help me go deeper with the Lord.

During the first few weeks, my plans fell nicely into place, with a couple of nagging exceptions. One was abdominal discomfort. Finally, about a month into my break, I visited my doctor.

He checked me out thoroughly, poking me in all the painful places and running a battery of tests. Finally he announced his diagnosis: "You have an ulcer," he said. "That's the source of your pain."

"You're kidding," I responded, both surprised and relieved that my condition wasn't more serious. "I've never had anything like this before."

"Well," my doctor continued, "ulcers are pretty common these days, with so much busyness and stress. How's your work going at church? Are you under an unusual amount of pressure these days?"

Sheepishly I answered, "You may not believe this, but my answer is no. In fact, I'm in the second month of a sabbatical. I've never felt less pressure from work in my life. It looks as if I'd better get back to work soon, for the sake of my health. All this rest is killing me!"

At that moment I thought, *A sabbatical seemed like a good idea, but now, who knows?*

The other nagging exception to my sabbatical-is-going-well rule had to do with my daily psalm reading. Praying a psalm each day had seemed like such a spiritual thing to do, but soon I began to feel terribly unspiritual because, frankly, I just didn't connect with many of the early psalms. I began happily enough with the encouragement of Psalm 1 to "delight...in the law of the LORD" (verse 2). But praise, which, given my experience in worship, seemed to be the major theme of the Psalms, hardly appeared in my first week's reading. In fact, among the first twenty psalms, only two focus primarily on praising God (Psalms 8 and 18).

Thirteen of these twenty psalms, however, overflow with self-centered requests, including several insolent demands that God get up and get going.[8] Almost half of the first twenty psalms are laments, to use the language of biblical scholarship. Normal folk would call them complaints against God. Sometimes the unhappy psalmist seems even to question God's faithfulness:

> How long, O LORD? Will you forget me forever?
>> How long will you hide your face from me?
> How long must I bear pain in my soul,
>> and have sorrow in my heart all day long?
> How long shall my enemy be exalted over me? (Psalm 13:1-2)

As I waded through this mire, I kept tripping over a peculiar preoccupation with wicked people and enemies (in seventeen of the first twenty psalms). These are folk I usually don't consider in my morning devotions. Moreover, some of what is said about these foes offended my Christian sensibilities. Was I really supposed to delight in the fact that God "will rain coals of fire and sulfur" on the wicked (Psalm 11:6)? How could I ask the God whose Son died for sinners to "break the arm of the wicked and evildoers" (Psalm 10:15)?

Three weeks into my sabbatical, I began to question the value of praying through the Psalms. I had expected this to enrich my relationship with God, but in predictable and comfortable ways. I looked forward to reveling in praise and adoration, not in supplication and complaint.

But as I continued praying these raw expressions of real life by using the words of the psalmists, I began to feel intrigued about what I was praying. How different the Psalms sounded from my usual prayers! How bold, surprising, and unsettling! Just maybe they would help my relationship with God to be less boring.

Anatomy of the Soul

By God's grace, my trek through the Psalms was timed perfectly, though I couldn't see this at first. During the early days of my sabbatical, I needed to learn to pray in the mode of the early psalms. Because of the physical suffering brought on by my ulcer, I found myself, like the psalmists, crying out to God for help and healing. My all-too-real enemies were not other people, but rather physical pain and especially the fear it instilled in me.

Before I went to the doctor, I worried incessantly about my stomach. Not only did I feel discomfort, but my symptoms were nearly identical to those that had plagued my dad when he was about my age. His illness, it turned out, was terminal cancer. The fear of cancer haunted me, especially when abdominal pain woke me in the dark of night.

One particular night was the worst. A sharp pain roused me from sleep, yet my emotional torment was worse than the physical. No matter how hard I tried to escape from fear's grasp, I felt sure I would die from cancer just like my father. I envisioned my wife without her husband and my young children without their father. I was terrified.

Even in that desperate moment, I still held back in my prayers. How could I be honest about my fears when they so clearly reflected my lack of trust in God? How could I tell him how disappointed I was in him? How could I say to the Lord, "Help me!" when I wasn't sure he even wanted to?

After all, he had let my father die from cancer. Finally, in my desperation, I remembered one of the distressing psalms I had read. Switching on the light and grabbing my Bible, I turned to Psalm 6. Here was a psalm that expressed what I felt but couldn't find the words to say:

> Be gracious to me, O LORD, for I am languishing;
>> O LORD, heal me, for my bones are shaking with terror.
> My soul also is struck with terror,
>> while you, O LORD—how long?
> Turn, O LORD, save my life;
>> deliver me for the sake of your steadfast love....
> I am weary with my moaning;
>> every night I flood my bed with tears;
>> I drench my couch with my weeping. (Psalm 6:2-4,6)

As I prayed this psalm, I didn't feel overwhelming peace or physical relief. But something profound happened inside. I stopped pretending that my need for relief could be expressed modestly and politely. I trusted my Lord enough to let him in on my despair, my anger, my fear, and my disappointment in him. By the power of God's Word in Psalm 6, I was unleashed before God, free to share myself with him, no holds barred.

Through praying this psalm I saw myself as I truly was: needier than I liked to admit, more fearful than I deemed acceptable, and famished for God. I understood why John Calvin called the Psalms "An Anatomy of all the Parts of the Soul." He noted that in this unique book "the Holy Spirit has here drawn to life all the griefs, sorrows, fears, doubts, hopes, cares, perplexities, in short, all the distracting emotions" that plague our minds. Yet Calvin did not see the Psalms as an invitation to introspection so much as to honest prayer in which we hold back "none of the many infirmities to which we are subject, and of the many vices with which we abound."[9]

In short, the Psalms teach us to "pour out [our] heart" to the Lord (Psalm 62:8). I began to learn that lesson during the initial days of my sabbatical. Since then I have continued to pray through the Psalms regularly, both in private and in groups. In my daily devotions, in weekly staff meetings, and in weekly prayer meetings with the elders from my church, I read a psalm in prayer. As a result, my prayers and those of my colleagues have become more honest, more probing, and more vital. Our relationships with the living God have taken on new life, more like intimate fellowship than a business partnership.

Our Honest Need

Let's face reality: You and I need a deeper, more expansive relationship with God. He desires completely unfettered intimacy with us. He has invited us to come boldly into his presence, sharing our selves with no holds barred. It's understandable that we're reluctant to do this, so God has given us the Psalms.

In each of the following chapters, I will explore one facet of our communication with God (asking, remembering, worshiping, thanking, and so forth), linking prayer with a model found in the Psalms. Some of the chapters will explore dimensions of prayer that may be unfamiliar to you (remembering, silence, revenge). Other chapters will delve into familiar expressions of prayer but will help you go deeper than you have gone before.

At the end of each chapter, I'll suggest an exercise or two to help you put into immediate practice what you have just learned from the Psalms. These exercises will be suitable for private and corporate prayer. I strongly urge you to do both.

If at any time as you're reading you feel a need to pray, then *please put down the book and start praying.* Remember: Although this book focuses on prayer, it's really a book about our relationship with God. Though I have written this book to help you pray more freely, I pray that at the end of the day, it will help you echo the confession of my friend Ben Patterson: *"I'm not into prayer, I'm into God!"*[10]

Who Holds Whom...and How?

In prayer we hold on to God, not letting go until he blesses us. The multiple dimensions of prayer are like wrestling holds, and we are free to use them all.

But praying involves other kinds of holding as well. Sometimes when we pray, we are "like a weaned child with its mother." We hold on to God, not as a wrestler grasps an opponent, but as a "calmed and quieted" child hugs a parent (Psalm 131:2). Like David, sometimes we grab on to God in prayer, but at other times our prayer is more like an embrace.

Embracing, like wrestling, takes two. The Psalms portray God as One who extends his strong arms to lift us up when we have fallen and to hold us even when we foolishly push him away:

> I was stupid and ignorant;
>> I was like a brute beast toward you.
> Nevertheless I am continually with you;
>> you hold my right hand. (Psalm 73:22-23)

In fact, we can never escape from God's loving grasp:

> If I take the wings of the morning
>> and settle at the farthest limits of the sea,
> even there your hand shall lead me,
>> and your right hand shall hold me fast. (Psalm 139:9-10)

Caught in the secure grip of God's powerful right hand, we delight in him:

> You show me the path of life.
>> In your presence there is fullness of joy;
>> in your right hand are pleasures forevermore. (Psalm 16:11)

The Psalms help us embrace the Lord more freely and fervently. They give us words to adore God, and they reveal a God worthy of unabashed adoration. But the Psalms also help us draw near to the God who holds us not only as a Wrestler but also as a loving Parent. In these ancient Hebrew prayers, we will meet once again the God whom Jesus revealed to be a compassionate, forgiving Father who throws his arms around us and welcomes us home (see Luke 15:20). "Lord, through all the generations you have been our home!" (Psalm 90:1, NLT).

Come home to God! Approach his throne of grace with boldness! Share your whole self with him! Allow him to hold you with a love that will never let you go!

An Exercise in Praying the Psalms

Start today praying through the book of Psalms, one chapter a day.[11] How do you pray a psalm? Some passages make this easy since they address God directly. Other passages don't speak to God, but they, too, can be read prayerfully. As you read—and I recommend reading aloud, if possible—let God be your primary audience.

Also, let the Spirit of God be your guide. Read with an eye to the text and an ear to the Spirit. You'll find that the Lord will speak to you, maybe through a word or a phrase, maybe through an image or a paragraph, maybe through the theme of the psalm. Read each psalm more than once, perhaps beginning with a quick read to get an overview of the chapter. Then read again, slowly, meditatively, aloud. Linger over words and phrases that resonate with your soul. Offer your reading to God as a prayer and attend to the inner voice of the Spirit.[12]

Praying the Psalms isn't the same as studying them, though the two disciplines go hand in hand. When we pray the Psalms, we aren't so much grappling with their meaning as with the God they reveal. We're speaking to God and listening to what he says through Word and Spirit.

If you find the ideas or phrases of a psalm confusing, you may wish to consult a study Bible or a commentary. I have been especially helped by the classic commentary by John Calvin and a much more recent commentary by Don Williams.[13] Both combine scholarly observation with spiritual insight. But if you're like me, you can get so wrapped up in figuring out the meaning of a psalm that you end up forgetting to pray it. So watch out, and remember the wise counsel of Eugene Peterson: "We don't learn the Psalms until we are praying them."[14]

Peterson also has strong opinions about the necessity of praying the Psalms with other believers. "Prayer is not a private exercise," he insists, "but a family convocation."[15] Though Peterson's either-or approach, which he later qualifies, might be too stark, he is right to urge us to pray the Psalms in community. Given our privatistic tendencies, Peterson's rhetoric ought to shock us into making sure we share our daily prayers with others. Small groups, prayer partnerships, Sunday-school classes, families, worship services—all these "congregations" and many more deserve to be enriched through the regular praying of the Psalms.

One of the easiest things about this exercise is its starting point. You don't have to wonder where to begin. Simply turn to Psalm 1 and start praying.

Hear a just cause, O LORD; attend to my cry;
    give ear to my prayer from lips free of deceit.
From you let my vindication come;
    let your eyes see the right.

If you try my heart, if you visit me by night,
    if you test me, you will find no wickedness in me;
    my mouth does not transgress.
As for what others do, by the word of your lips
    I have avoided the ways of the violent.
My steps have held fast to your paths;
    my feet have not slipped.

I call upon you, for you will answer me, O God;
    incline your ear to me, hear my words.
Wondrously show your steadfast love,
    O savior of those who seek refuge
    from their adversaries at your right hand.

Guard me as the apple of the eye;
    hide me in the shadow of your wings,
from the wicked who despoil me,
    my deadly enemies who surround me.
They close their hearts to pity;
    with their mouths they speak arrogantly.
They track me down; now they surround me;
    they set their eyes to cast me to the ground.
They are like a lion eager to tear,
    like a young lion lurking in ambush.

Rise up, O LORD, confront them, overthrow them!
    By your sword deliver my life from the wicked,
from mortals—by your hand, O LORD—
    from mortals whose portion in life is in this world.
May their bellies be filled with what you have stored up for them;
    may their children have more than enough;
    may they leave something over to their little ones.
As for me, I shall behold your face in righteousness;
    when I awake I shall be satisfied, beholding your likeness.

—PSALM 17:1-15

HEY, GOD—GET UP!

Prayer of Asking

A sking. I don't like to do it. I'm not talking just about the cases where insecure men like me struggle to request assistance, like when I'm befuddled in a hardware store. My resistance to asking goes much deeper. I've been request-challenged for as long as I can remember.

What's the source of my emotional reticence? I've thought about this a lot. Is it pride, fear of rejection, or some other defense mechanism? Frankly, I'm not sure. Bottom line: I'm just not comfortable asking people for things.

So it must have been God's sense of humor that paired me with my college roommate Henry. He had *no* problem with asking. In fact, he relished the challenge of asking people for favors *especially* when he had little chance of getting what he wanted. If a sign in a store said "No public restroom," Henry would ask the clerk, "Could I please use your restroom?" When he did this I wanted to melt into the floor. But I was amazed at how often he ended up receiving the thing he asked for.

One Friday evening Henry and I were waiting in line to see a movie when he spotted a giant poster promoting the film.

"That's a cool poster," he said. "I want it."

"Well, that's too bad," I responded, "because they don't give those things away."

"They might," Henry said. "I'll just ask the theater manager if I can have it."

Here we go again, I thought as I imagined the manager laughing in our faces. Of course Henry wouldn't mind the rejection. But I, his loyal sidekick, would feel enough humiliation for both of us.

Henry was already approaching the manager. "Say, I like that movie poster out there. Could I have it when you're done with it?"

"We don't give out the posters," the manager responded curtly, just as I had sagely foretold. Then, inexplicably, he seemed to waver for a moment. "But…," he said hesitantly, "I don't see why we can't make an exception in this case. If you come back in a week, after the run of the film is over, I'll give you the poster."

"Thanks," beamed Henry, delighted by his improbable victory and pleased, no doubt, that he had once again revealed the folly of my fear. Of course, experiences like this egged him on to further exploits in audacious asking—to his delight and my chagrin.

Asking Like David

Henry reminds me of David because the prolific psalmist majored in asking. Almost half of the biblical psalms are attributed to David,[1] and these overflow with requests—for help, protection, deliverance, healing, and so on. Take Psalm 17. In fifteen brief verses, David made at least seventeen requests of the Lord, including "hear a just cause," "attend to my cry," "give ear to my prayer," "let my vindication come," and so forth.[2] David was clearly not request-challenged. He knew the Lord so well that he felt free to ask him for just about anything. Now that's freedom I crave. I'll bet you do too.

If we want to experience this sort of freedom as we deepen our relationship with God, Psalm 17 is a good place to start. It's a basic, straightforward prayer. Through careful study of this psalm, we'll learn how to pray—in this case, how to ask—like David. More important, we'll begin to experience the intimacy David enjoyed in his relationship with God, an intimacy that enabled him to ask simply, repeatedly, and even boldly.

Ask Simply

Asking doesn't require a large vocabulary, persuasive arguments, or carefully devised strategies. Psalm 17 abounds with uncomplicated requests. Without a preamble of praise or a declaration of divine glory,[3] David jumped right in: "Hear a just cause, O LORD; attend to my cry; give ear to my prayer from lips free of deceit" (verse 1). This psalm hints at the crisis that motivated David to pray with such passion. He was being threatened by enemies who sought to injure him through false accusation, if not physical violence. Thus, David asked God to hear him, defend him, save him, and judge his opponents.

To be sure, at times we will frame our supplications with praise and thanksgiving. The apostle Paul counsels us to let our requests be made known to God "with thanksgiving" (Philippians 4:6). But Psalm 17 gives us permission to ask simply, without worrying that our naked requests are unworthy of God. In fact, too much attention to using just the right words builds a barrier between us and God, not a bridge.[4]

As a pastor I often meet with people who are just learning how to pray. "I don't know the right words to say," they explain. I encourage these folk—as I urge you right now—to forget about seeking the right words. Just talk to God in words that flow from your heart. "Genuine and earnest prayer," John Calvin advised, "proceeds first from a sense of our need."[5] Simply lay your needs—not highfalutin verbiage or theological sophistication—before the God who seeks relationship with you. The Psalms teach that prayer is "sputtering our unrehearsed answers to the God who calls us into a life of covenant," to use Eugene Peterson's vivid language.[6] God prefers it when we sputter, because it shows the desperate need we are admitting to him. The Holy Spirit will help you pray, not with perfect phrasing, but "with sighs too deep for words" (Romans 8:26).

By praying the Psalms—reading them as prayers—we will learn a direct, unrehearsed, and inspired language of prayer. We will discover words with which to express the deepest desires of our soul. But even more important, we will learn to pour out our hearts freely to the Lord because he is our refuge, a safe place where we can be our true selves without pretense (see Psalm 62:8).

King David's requests to the King of the universe throughout Psalm 17 don't sound like official entreaties from a subject to a king so much as unsophisticated demands from a child to a parent. David said to the Lord, "Bend down and listen as I pray" (verse 6, NLT). Kings don't bend down to hear the requests of their groveling subjects, but loving parents gladly stoop to hear what their small children are asking. Parents don't demand that their children get all the words right, either.

Though David's prayers are often childlike, he did not go nearly as far as Jesus, who invites us to address God in prayer as "our Father" (see, for example, Matthew 6:9). Nevertheless, the psalmist modeled intimacy with God that came to full fruition in the ministry of Jesus. Following in David's footsteps, Jesus teaches us to pray primarily by offering simple, childlike requests: "Our Father in heaven… Your kingdom come. Your will be done.… Give us this day our daily bread."[7] Therefore, we have even greater reason than David to pray simply, as children who tell our heavenly Father what's on our hearts without worrying about impressing God with our eloquence.

When my daughter, Kara, was a toddler, she fabricated the word *uppy*. It meant "I want you to pick me up, please, Daddy." Whenever Kara came to me, arms raised as if in prayer, and said "uppy," do you think I spurned her because she didn't use proper English? Do you think I waited until she could address me with appropriate respect? Hardly! I loved it when my daughter cried "uppy," and I was able to swoop her up into my arms and hug her. How much more delight must our heavenly Father feel when we call out to him in heartfelt simplicity! Jesus reminds us of this truth: "If you then, who are evil, know how to give good gifts to your children, *how much more* will your Father in heaven give good things to those who ask him!" (Matthew 7:11). Did you catch that? *"To those who ask him,"* God will give good things. "Ask, and it will be given you," Jesus promises (Matthew 7:7). It's really that simple.

Ask Repeatedly

My Hebrew teacher in graduate school was a brilliant linguist but not a big fan of the Psalms. "I'm mystified about why people are so excited about the Psalms," he once lamented in class. "In the whole book there are only about a dozen ideas. And these keep repeating over and over and over." Although I'm one of those mysterious people who love the Psalms, my professor did have a point (well, sort of). There is ample repetition in the whole corpus of the Psalms. Often within one psalm we find the same ideas being repeated.

The repetitiveness of the Psalms reflects, in part, the nature of Hebrew poetry. Whereas we write poems by utilizing rhythm and rhyme, Hebrew poets employed parallelism, composing one line and then following it with another that conveyed a similar idea in different words. We see this in the first verse of Psalm 17:

Line 1: Hear a just cause, O LORD;

Line 2: attend to my cry;

Line 3: give ear to my prayer from lips free of deceit.

But poetic parallelism alone does not completely account for the recurrent nature of David's supplications. Five times in Psalm 17 he asked the Lord in varying words to hear his prayer (verses 1,6). Five times he requested that justice be meted out to his enemies (verses 13-14). Clearly David felt free to ask for what he needed, not just simply but repeatedly as well.

Some Christians feel uncomfortable with repetition. I once heard a preacher who actually instructed his congregation not to ask God for something more than once. Duplicating requests, he argued, is evidence of our failure to trust God. If we have genuine faith, we'll ask for something once and only once—not only in a particular prayer but in all of our prayers put together. If you have cancer, for example, you shouldn't ask for healing but one time. Every recurrent plea shows how little you trust the Lord.

This preacher should have spent less time using his flawed logic to figure out how to pray and more time reading the Psalms (not to mention the Gospels). You can't read one psalm, not to mention the whole collection, without marveling at the freedom of the psalmists to ask again and again for what they need.[8]

Though I reject the pray-only-once advice, I do appreciate that preacher's concern. After all, if God hears every one of our prayers, why would he encourage recurrent supplication? Doesn't the Almighty get just a little tired of hearing the same old thing again and again? I quickly lose patience with my children when they persist in asking for favors after I've declined to grant them. By the third or fourth "Daddy, can we go to Ruby's for dinner?" I'm about ready to ask the Lord to "deliver my life from the wicked" (Psalm 17:13).

Scripture never explains why God promotes repeated supplication, so please take the following suggestion with a grain of salt. It makes sense that if

God doesn't need to hear our redundant requests for his own sake, since he knows what we need even before we ask the first time, then perhaps repetition in prayer is more for *our* sake. I know this is true for me.

Recently I found myself in a very dicey situation at church, one that required far more wisdom than I could muster. For months I prayed about this crisis, pouring out my heart to God. During that time I uttered the request, "Help me, Lord," at least a thousand times—literally. I have no doubt that God got the point the first time, but I needed to keep saying these words because, as I did, God touched my heart. What began almost as an order to God, "Help me, Lord, by doing what I demand!" in time became an offer of submission, "Help me, Lord, to know your will and do it." What started in desperation—"Help me, Lord, because I'm scared to death about what's hap-pening"—became a calm recognition of God's sovereignty—"Help me, Lord, because you alone are my strength." By praying the same prayer over and over, I finally allowed my heart to open to God's grace so that I might receive "the peace of God, which surpasses all understanding" (Philippians 4:7). So, though I don't believe God needed to hear more than one "Help me, Lord," I needed to say this myriad times before I was ready to receive the help he wanted to give me.

Ask Boldly

The simplicity and repetition of David's prayer in Psalm 17 reflect his bold-ness before God. He never spoke in the manner required of a subject before a sovereign, as illustrated by Queen Esther before her husband, King Ahasuerus: "If it pleases the king, and if I have won his favor, and if the thing seems right before the king, and I have his approval, let an order be written…" (Esther 8:5). David, on the contrary, approached the King of kings with a series of blunt, bold requests: Hear! Attend! Give ear! Vindicate me!

Many of the requests in Psalm 17 are imperatives. In Hebrew they look at first like commands, as if David was telling God what to do. But Hebrew imperatives, when they come from a subordinate to a superior, convey respect and honor, not insolence. When David prayed, "Guard me as the apple of the eye" (verse 8), he was humbly asking for divine protection, not giving the Lord an order.

But then we come to verse 13: "Rise up, O LORD, confront [my enemies], overthrow them!" "Rise up" sounds an awful lot like what a king would yell to a lazy servant. Did David believe that God was sleeping? Did he envision himself as a divine alarm clock? Apparently so, and not just in Psalm 17. In Psalm 35 David shouted to the Lord, "Wake up! Bestir yourself for my defense" (verse 23). Other psalm writers echoed David's brashness. Take Psalm 44, for example, where the sons of Korah exclaimed:

Rouse yourself! Why do you sleep, O Lord?
　　Awake, do not cast us off forever!
Why do you hide your face?
　　Why do you forget our affliction and oppression?
For we sink down to the dust;
　　our bodies cling to the ground.
Rise up, come to our help.
　　Redeem us for the sake of your steadfast love. (verses 23-26)

Do you ever talk to the Lord this way? Should we be telling God to get up and get going, as if he has dozed off?

I relate to the desperation behind the imperative "Get up, Lord" when I remember my experience with nightmares as a young child. Upon waking in the dark, I'd be terribly frightened. So I'd call out to my parents: "Mommy! Daddy! Help me! Get up!" My bold imperative "Get up!" flowed not from a sense of haughtiness but from desperation. I didn't censor my speech but simply shouted out my needs with the first words I could utter.

As a grownup I do censor my speech, all the time. That's part of what maturity requires. But, unfortunately, I sometimes squelch my communication with God in a way that blocks genuine relationship with him. I often want to censor what flows from my heart because it's so messy. In times of fearful desperation, I've wanted to cry out to God, "Rouse yourself! Why do you sleep, O Lord?" But then I catch myself. *Of course God isn't sleeping*, I reason. *He doesn't need to wake up. Besides, who am I to say such things to the Lord?* So I end up with some insipid confession of God's care for me, rather than the fearful and frustrated but altogether genuine cry of my heart. Is

God, who looks upon the heart, fooled by any of this? No. Am I doing God, or myself, any favors by limiting our communication with such sanitized prayers? No.

The Psalms model not just freedom but boldness. They teach us to speak to God in ways that would seem utterly inappropriate if they were not right there in the middle of the Bible. From God's point of view, it's okay—no, it's absolutely right—to communicate what's in our heart, even if it doesn't always jibe with the best systematic theology. There'll be plenty of opportunity to clean things up later. First, God wants our heart.

"But," you might object, "there's no way I could say things like this to God. I can't imagine being so brash." I understand because I'm just like you. So what can you do? Praying the Psalms on a regular basis can transform your personal prayers. If you can't speak certain words to God, pray God's own words back to him. As you pray through the Psalms, you'll get plenty of practice telling God to rise up. Furthermore, in times of desperation, turn to the Psalms and let them express what's in your heart. There's untold power in praying the Word of God.

Why We Can Ask Boldly

If you are overly hesitant to ask boldly, you need more than the example of the Psalms, however. You need to know the God of the Psalms more intimately. Bold supplication is our response to God's own character and invitation.

We pray hesitantly because our knowledge of God is deficient. We often relate to him as if he were the kitchen master in Oliver Twist's workhouse. He's the guy who faced the famished Oliver when the lad had the audacity to ask the unthinkable: "Please, sir, I want some more." Astonished, the master said, "What?!" To which Oliver replied, "Please, sir, I want some more." Immediately the horrified master bonked the hungry lad on the head with a ladle, grabbed him to prevent his escape, and turned him over to the workhouse officials, who put Oliver up for sale.[9] If God is anything like this, then we'd be fools to offer such bold requests.

But the Psalms reveal a very different God. In Psalm 17, for example,

David evinced confidence in God's goodness: "I call upon you, *for you will answer me,* O God" (verse 6). No fear of ladle-bonking here. Just steady faith in a God who hears and answers prayer. David continued:

> Wondrously show your steadfast love,
>> O savior of those who seek refuge
>> from their adversaries at your right hand. (verse 7)

The Lord is, first of all, the God who shows "steadfast love." This English phrase is a translation of the Hebrew word *chesed,* which is often rendered "lovingkindness" or "unfailing love." *Chesed* is God's covenant love given to Israel and to all who enter into a committed relationship with him. Because our God is a God of *chesed,* we can be confident that nothing in all creation can separate us from his love (see Romans 8:31-39).

Divine *chesed* is not theoretical, but actual and historical. From David's point of view, it was revealed to Israel in the exodus from Egypt, in the forging of the covenant at Mount Sinai, and in countless other acts of God. The psalmist's understanding of this actualized *chesed* lies behind his double request in Psalm 17:8: "Guard me as the apple of the eye; hide me in the shadow of your wings." David didn't make up these poetic phrases. Rather, he borrowed them from Moses's celebration of God's covenant faithfulness to Israel:

> [The LORD] sustained [Jacob] in a desert land,
>> in a howling wilderness waste;
> he shielded him, cared for him,
>> guarded him as the apple of his eye.
> As an eagle stirs up its nest,
>> and hovers over its young;
> as it spreads its wings, takes them up,
>> and bears them aloft on its pinions,
> the LORD alone guided him;
>> no foreign god was with him. (Deuteronomy 32:10-12)

Thus, in Psalm 17 David was not praying to some god of his own imagination, but to the covenant-making God of Israel, the One who revealed his nature as a faithful, gracious, protective God.

David brought his supplication before the God he knew as the "savior of those who seek refuge from their adversaries" (verse 7). Therefore he could ask with confidence, "Wondrously show your steadfast love" (verse 7). He wasn't saying, "Do something new for me," but "Be for me the God you have always been." David's boldness came not from inappropriate brashness but from his knowledge of God.

As Christians we know God as Savior in a way that surpasses David's comprehension. We are the ones who are invited into God's chamber: "Let us therefore approach the throne of grace *with boldness*" (Hebrews 4:16). Because of what Jesus accomplished as our Great High Priest, we have unparalleled freedom in God's presence. Consequently, we ought to *exceed* the boldness we see in the Psalms. God is our Father who rushes to embrace us. Jesus the Son is the High Priest who enables us to approach God's throne with boldness. And God the Holy Spirit helps us in our weakness to pray from the depths of our heart.[10] The more we know God, the more we will be empowered to pray boldly as we stand in the righteousness of Christ.

The Surprising Purpose of Asking

We ask so that God will answer, right? Isn't that the point of laying our requests before him? This is why we beg God to do what we desire, or at least that's the common understanding of prayer. In Psalm 17 when David prayed for vindication, protection, and deliverance, he did so because he was seeking—you guessed it—vindication, protection, and deliverance. This isn't rocket science.

Maybe not, but the deeper purpose of "asking" prayers isn't as obvious as it appears. Without a doubt David sought God's help. Encircled by his enemies, he begged the Lord to deliver him. But pay close attention to the last verse in Psalm 17. After fourteen verses filled with urgent personal requests, David's tone and focus changed dramatically at the end of the prayer: "As for me, I shall behold your face in righteousness; when I awake I shall be satisfied, beholding your likeness" (verse 15).

In contrast to his enemies—mortals who seek worldly fulfillment—David found ultimate satisfaction only in God. The verb "to be satisfied" in verse 15 appears in verse 14 in the phrase "may their children *have more than enough*." Elsewhere David used this same verb to express his utter delight in God: "My soul *is satisfied* as with a rich feast" (Psalm 63:5). Physical satisfaction comes with that last bite of pumpkin pie after Thanksgiving dinner. Spiritual satisfaction comes when we see God and dwell in his presence. God alone fills our souls with more than enough.

Psalm 17 demonstrates a deeper purpose for asking in prayer. When the dust of David's persecution settles, he will be satisfied not merely with vindication but with seeing the face of God. Of course, like David, we ask in prayer because we want God's answers. But more profoundly, we ask because asking brings us near to God. When we approach the throne of grace boldly, seeking mercy and grace in our time of need, we get more than what we came for. We receive both God's help *and* God's presence. We ask in prayer because we need answers. But we ask because, most of all, we need God. Supplication opens the doors to deeper relationship with the Lord.[11]

This reminds me of an experience I had with my son, Nathan, when he was four years old. One night he crept into my bedroom and woke me up. "Dad," he whispered, "I'm scared. Can you come sleep with me?" Dutifully I dragged myself out of bed and squeezed into Nathan's little bunk until he fell back to sleep.

The next night, in the middle of my sweet dreams, I heard, "Dad, I'm scared. Can you come sleep with me?" Once again I trudged off to attend to his need for comfort. Now Nathan was on a roll. By about the fifth night of being awakened, I started wondering about his "I'm scared" line, because he didn't seem particularly upset. I began to suspect that something else was motivating his request.

The following evening as I tucked Nathan into bed, I said, "You know, buddy, how you're coming in every night because you're scared? Well, I want you to know that I'm always there for you if you're frightened. You can always come and get me. But, Nathan, you don't have to be scared to wake me up. Sometimes you might just need a hug, and that's okay. So you don't have to pretend you're scared if you're really not. Do you understand?"

Nathan seemed to get the point, so we said our prayers, and he soon fell asleep.

Several hours later I was once again wakened by a plaintive little voice. But this time it said, "Dad, I'm *not* scared, but could you come sleep with me anyway?"

What Nathan needed was not my help so much as me. Asking was a way for him to draw near to me and enjoy our relationship. So it is with us and God. Even though we sometimes think that getting answers to prayer is the main and most important point, fellowship with God is even sweeter. It satisfies most of all.

My friend Dee has an extensive ministry of visitation. In the course of her care for sick and shut-in people, she began visiting a man named Harold. He was getting on in years and was struggling with an excruciating disease. Dee would often join him in asking God for physical healing, but those prayers seemed to receive a big fat no from the Lord. Yet Harold and Dee kept on asking.

Because of his illness, Harold started spending more time in prayer and Bible study. Though he had been a Christian for years, Harold had spent most of his time in worldly pursuits. But pain reoriented his priorities. At first his interest in God was focused on his desire for relief from suffering—understandably so. But over time he began to delight more and more in God's presence.

During one of her visits, Dee asked Harold, "If you had the choice today between being well again but going back to being far from God or suffering as you are now but staying close to God, what would you choose?" He answered, "The second, no question about it. Being close to God is far better than being physically well." Like David, Harold realized that true satisfaction comes not in getting our prayers answered but in knowing intimately the One who answers prayers, even when his answer is no.

Open Your Heart to the God Who Seeks the Real You

People often ask me why God wants us to make requests in prayer. If he knows what's best, they wonder, then why doesn't he just go ahead and do it? What's the point of his waiting for us to ask?

There is a mystery in supplication that exceeds our understanding. The Sovereign Lord, the One who is all-knowing, all-wise, and all-powerful, has chosen to include us among his advisors. He not only listens to our prayers, he acts in response to them.

Why? Partly, I think, to remind us how much we need his help. If God automatically did what was right without us asking, we'd figure that the world simply works perfectly and that God is neither active nor necessary. Supplication helps us recognize our need for God and marvel at his power when he answers prayer.

Supplication also allows us to participate in God's work in the cosmos. He placed us in his world to take care of it and to work within it.[12] Prayer is an essential aspect of our stewardship and labor.[13]

But even beyond helping us realize our need for God and allowing us to be his co-workers, God wants us to pray because he wants *us*. While it's true that supplication helps us draw near to God, and this satisfies our souls, it's just as true that our supplication delights the heart of God.

Scripture reveals a God who seeks relationship with us. He is the Good Shepherd who searches for the lost sheep and, when he finds it, lays it on his shoulders and rejoices (see Luke 15:3-7). God is the waiting Father who runs to embrace his lost child. Then he throws a lavish party to celebrate the child's return (see Luke 15:11-32). God seeks our worship, even as he seeks us (see John 4:23-24). Most of all, God is the One who, through Christ, died on the cross, bearing our separation from him, so that we might be restored to intimate relationship with him (see 2 Corinthians 5:21).

Thus God wants us to pray, not only so that he might bless us with answers, but also so that he might bless us with his presence—and so that we might bless him with our presence. Supplication leads us to the throne of grace so that we might embrace the One who sits on the throne, and so that he might embrace us, to our mutual delight.

As you read the story of my son who woke me up in the middle of the night, you might have wondered why I didn't just send him back to bed, at least after the second night. Maybe you thought I was being too much of a softy. And maybe I was. But I must confess that I roused myself from sleep and cuddled with my son not just to satisfy his longing but to satisfy mine.

The moments I spent hugging him in his little bed were some of the most precious moments of my life. His midnight requests ended up satisfying not just his soul but mine as well.

Though my heart is only a dim reflection of our heavenly Father's heart, I believe that my desire for relationship with Nathan is in some tiny way like God's desire for relationship with you and me. Take my yearning for intimacy with my son, multiply it by a thousand, and then you're *just beginning* to fathom God's desire for his children. God wants you to pray because God wants *you*. He has given you the Psalms because he wants you to draw near to him. He wants you to ask in prayer, with no holds barred, because he desires to bless you and, more wonderfully still, because he desires relationship with the real you.

So go ahead and ask. Ask simply! Ask repeatedly! Ask boldly! Draw near to God and don't hold back.

An Exercise in Prayer of Asking

Read Psalm 17 carefully, prayerfully. Try to put yourself in David's place. Feel his desperation, his desire for vindication, his yearning for God. Attend to his faith in the One who is "savior of those who seek refuge" (verse 7). As you pray meditatively through this psalm, let the words of verse 15 sink into your soul: "As for me, I shall behold your face in righteousness; when I awake I shall be satisfied, beholding your likeness." Could you pray like this? Ask the Lord to increase your desire for him.

After you have prayed Psalm 17, consider your own communication with God. Are you as free as David in your supplication? If not, what is keeping you from praying with no holds barred? Are there certain things you'd like to say to God but haven't done so? On the basis of Psalm 17, lay yourself and your needs honestly before God. Have the confidence to tell him anything, everything.

This psalm inspires corporate prayer as well as private prayer. In a gathering with other believers, pray through Psalm 17 and allow this text to guide group supplication.

O give thanks to the LORD, call on his name,
    make known his deeds among the peoples.
Sing to him, sing praises to him;
    tell of all his wonderful works.
Glory in his holy name;
    let the hearts of those who seek the LORD rejoice.
Seek the LORD and his strength;
    seek his presence continually.
Remember the wonderful works he has done,
    his miracles, and the judgments he uttered,
O offspring of his servant Abraham,
    children of Jacob, his chosen ones.

      —PSALM 105:1-6

Both we and our ancestors have sinned;
    we have committed iniquity, have done wickedly.
Our ancestors, when they were in Egypt,
    did not consider your wonderful works;
they did not remember the abundance of your steadfast love,
    but rebelled against the Most High at the Red Sea.

      —PSALM 106:6-7

PRAYING LIKE ELEPHANTS

Prayer of Remembering

E lephants never forget, or so the saying goes. And some people never forget an elephant.

Late in the nineteenth century, master showman P. T. Barnum made a
small fortune charging people to see Jumbo, allegedly the world's largest elephant. But when a train crash tragically ended Jumbo's profitable life, Barnum
wasn't finished with the great beast. He had Jumbo stuffed and delivered to
Tufts University outside Boston, where Barnum was a trustee. For almost a
century Tufts students prized the mammoth mummy, which was displayed in
the student center, fittingly named Barnum Hall. In fact, they named themselves the Tufts Jumbos in honor of their beloved elephant.

But in 1975 a fire destroyed Barnum Hall. Jumbo seemed to meet his
final end in the conflagration. Yet, when the fire was extinguished, an enter-
prising assistant in the Tufts athletic department carefully gathered Jumbo's
charred remains, preserving them in an empty peanut-butter jar. To this day,
athletes at Tufts have not forgotten dear Jumbo. Before every big game, they
reverently rub his peanut-butter urn for good luck. Like the elephant for
which they are named, the Tufts Jumbos never forget.

And neither should we. I'm not getting sentimental about an elephant,
mind you. What we should never forget is not some dead elephant, but the
living God, the God of history, the God of our salvation.

Well, it's obvious that I should never forget about God, you may be thinking.
I agree it's obvious that we shouldn't, but it's also way too easy to forget him.

And we are not to just remember God; we are to remember his work in our lives. When was the last time you called to mind, while talking to God, many of the ways you have experienced his grace? Have you ever recounted in prayer God's saving works throughout history, beginning with Abraham, moving to the Exodus, and continuing throughout the biblical record? How often do you take time to do what the psalmist calls us to do?

> Seek the LORD and his strength;
>> seek his presence continually.
> *Remember the wonderful works he has done,*
>> his miracles, and the judgments he uttered. (Psalm 105:4-5)

If you're like most Christians I know, you do seek the Lord regularly, but you rarely remember—*really* remember—his wonderful works, miracles, and judgments. God might get a quick "thank you" in response to some fleeting recollection. But intentional, extended prayers of remembering just don't make it into the prayer repertoire of most believers. When we're wrestling with God in prayer, this is one of the "holds" we usually bar. Yet it's one we need to experience, especially in this day when forgetfulness of the past runs rampant.

WHAT IS PRAYER OF REMEMBERING?

In its simplest form, prayer of remembering tells God what he has done for us. We find a striking example in one of David's psalms:

> I will extol you, O LORD, for you have drawn me up,
>> and did not let my foes rejoice over me.
> O LORD my God, I cried to you for help,
>> and you have healed me.
> O LORD, you brought up my soul from Sheol,
>> restored me to life from among those gone down to the Pit....
> You have turned my mourning into dancing;
>> you have taken off my sackcloth
>> and clothed me with joy. (Psalm 30:1-3,11)

Here David remembered how God healed him from a life-threatening disease, restoring him to wholeness and joyful living. He provided the Lord with a detailed account of divine deliverance. David offered more than a rushed "Thanks, Lord, for healing me."

Though the Psalms teach us to recall before the Lord what he has done for us individually, they also expand our recollection to include his mighty works in biblical history. Three psalms in particular go to great lengths to chronicle God's salvation of Israel: Psalms 78, 105, and 106. Psalm 105, for example, begins with a call to worship that becomes a call to remember:

> O give thanks to the LORD, call on his name....
> *Remember* the wonderful works he has done,
>> his miracles, and the judgments he uttered,
> O offspring of his servant Abraham,
>> children of Jacob, his chosen ones (verses 1,5-6).

Then the psalm takes off in a flurry of recollection, devoting thirty-nine verses to a detailed recounting of God's relationship with Israel. These verses touch upon:

- God's establishing a covenant with Abraham (verses 7-11)
- God's protection of the wandering Israelites (verses 12-15)
- God's sovereignty over and blessing of Joseph (verses 16-22)
- God's blessing of Israel in Egypt as preparation for the Exodus (verses 23-25)
- God's deliverance from Egypt through Moses and the plagues (verses 26-36)
- God's care for Israel in the wilderness (verses 37-42)
- God's gift of the Promised Land to his people (verses 43-45)

Psalm 106 also recollects God's deliverance of Israel, with added emphasis on the sinfulness of the people. Time and again the Israelites failed to remember God's grace and so sinned against him:

> Both we and our ancestors have sinned;
>> we have committed iniquity, have done wickedly.

Our ancestors, when they were in Egypt,
    did not consider your wonderful works;
they did not remember the abundance of your steadfast love,
    but rebelled against the Most High at the Red Sea....

They made a calf at Horeb
    and worshiped a cast image.
They exchanged the glory of God
    for the image of an ox that eats grass.
They forgot God, their Savior,
    who had done great things in Egypt. (verses 6-7,19-21)

As a result of Israel's forgetful unfaithfulness, God finally delivered his people "into the hand of the nations" (verse 41). But he did not fully abandon them.

Nevertheless [the LORD] regarded their distress
    when he heard their cry.
For their sake he remembered his covenant,
    and showed compassion according to the abundance of his stead-
        fast love. (verses 44-45)

Prayers of remembrance focus upon God's gracious actions within history, but they do not sugarcoat the sorry record of human rebellion against the Lord. In fact, when contrasted with the dark backdrop of our forgetful rejection of God, his tenacious mercy shines even more brightly.

How We Offer Prayers of Remembrance

One of the best ways to start remembering in prayer is to be guided by Psalms 78, 105, and 106. If you read any of these psalms as a prayer, you'll begin to "remember the wonderful works" of the Lord (Psalm 105:5). If you adopt the discipline of reading a psalm a day, then at least six times each year you'll be led into prayers of remembrance.

The Psalms, however, only begin to recount God's saving works. We see in the Old Testament's images of salvation a preview of coming attractions, which were revealed centuries later in the person and work of Jesus Christ. The feature presentation is, of course, redemption through Jesus Christ. Thus, let the Old Testament psalms be a jumping-off point for your recollection. Take time to express prayerfully what God has done in Christ. Consider the wonders of Jesus's birth, his life, his proclamation of the kingdom, his love for the unlovely, his invitation for us to call God "Father," his sacrifice on the cross, and his resurrection on Easter. Don't rush through your remembrance, but allow sufficient time for the Spirit of God to bring to mind the "wonderful works" of God in Christ.

After recalling the works of God recorded in Scripture, you can follow the lead of Psalm 30 by remembering God's gracious deeds in your own life. Tell the Lord how he has rescued you not only from death into eternal life but from myriad problems, illnesses, and sins. Again, give this process the time it deserves. Full remembrance involves restful reflection, as we learn from Psalm 77:

> I will call to mind the deeds of the LORD;
>> I will remember your wonders of old.
> I will meditate on all your work,
>> and muse on your mighty deeds. (verses 11-12)

Many of us will find remembering our personal experiences of grace to be more emotionally moving than recounting the biblical history of salvation. But don't shortchange the broader remembrance of God's mighty works in the past. This establishes our personal experience upon the bedrock of divine revelation, refreshes us in the solidness of God's grace, and inspires us to consider aspects of our own experience that we might otherwise neglect.

To this point I have spoken as if you should offer prayers of remembering when you are alone with the Lord. Surely remembrance belongs in private devotions, but the principal context for remembering prayer is the gathered body of believers. In Psalm 105, for example, the call to "remember the wonderful works" of God is given to the "offspring of his servant Abraham, children of Jacob, his chosen ones" (verses 5-6). The psalm continues by affirming that the Lord is "*our* God"—the God not just of individuals but of the covenant people taken together (verse 7). The fact that Psalm 105 belongs primarily (but not exclusively) among the prayers of God's gathered people is seen in 1 Chronicles 16. Just after the ark of God arrived in Jerusalem, David appointed certain Levites to lead the people in singing praise to the Lord. And how did they begin? By reciting the first fifteen verses of Psalm 105. Remembering God lays the foundation for corporate worship.

I'm emphasizing the need for corporate remembrance because we might easily neglect the corporate in favor of the private. The pervasive tendency in Western Christianity is toward individualistic, even secretive prayer. Rightly, we understand that we can have a personal relationship with God through Christ. Wrongly, we assume that what is so personal must be essentially private. But from the biblical point of view, deeply personal faith must be shared among fellow believers. It is still "not good that the man should be alone" (Genesis 2:18). As I demonstrated in my book *After "I Believe,"* the full Christian life is intimate fellowship with God *and with God's people.*[1] This is especially true when it comes to prayer.

When we remember together the mighty works of God, we pray more deeply, more expansively, more joyfully. In 2002 my church celebrated its twenty-fifth anniversary. For a weekend we gathered to remember God's blessings and to celebrate his grace. How encouraged I was to hear from others how God had ministered to them during the past quarter century. How many times I was reminded by others of mercies I would have forgotten if left to my own devices. The focal point of our celebration was a two-hour worship service, which for Presbyterians might be an all-time record. With psalms, hymns, and spiritual songs we remembered God's "wonderful works" (Psalm 105:5). Our common recollection enriched our individual memory and enlivened our worship.

One of the chief ways we remember God's grace together is through reenactment. To the Israelites God gave the festival of Passover as "a day of remembrance" (Exodus 12:14) so that they might remember the Exodus through words and actions. By eating lamb, unleavened bread, and bitter herbs, God's people were to recall and relive their divine deliverance from Egypt. In the

Passover celebration we see a melding of ritual, recollection, and reenactment that brings God's salvation to life once again.

Likewise, Jesus gave us the celebration of Communion so that we might remember him.[2] We do this, in part, through symbolic reenactment of his death. We break bread that represents his broken body. We drink wine that signifies his shed blood. And we use words to interpret these symbols: "The Lord Jesus on the night when he was betrayed took a loaf of bread...." (1 Corinthians 11:23). The remembrance of the Lord's Supper is something we do together as the people of God. Our corporate sharing accentuates the personal power of the sacrament.

So it is with prayers of remembrance. Our private recollection is enhanced through our corporate remembering and reenacting.

The Rewards of Remembering

During the last three years, as I have prayed through the Psalms on a daily basis, I have discovered the rewards of prayers of remembrance. My relationship with God has been strengthened and stretched as I have prayed through Psalms 78, 105, and 106—and as I have allowed these psalms to inspire my personal devotion to God.

The rewards of remembrance are many. As you pray in this mode, I'm sure you'll be able to add to the following list of benefits.

We Are Anchored to the Real God

Remembering God gives us an anchor to the real God. It keeps us from drifting away from his true nature into heresies and vain inventions.

God is not some figment of our imagination. He is the God who has revealed himself in word and in deed, in Scripture and in history, and most of all in Jesus Christ, the Word made flesh. The Bible offers a divinely inspired, utterly trustworthy account of God's activity in the world. Thus, if we want to know the real God, we must turn to Scripture, where we discover not only truths about God's nature but also the true story of his mighty works. When we remember these works, we remember God and know him truthfully.

Seeking God in Scripture goes against the current of contemporary culture. The dominant desire today—even among Christians—is to know God immediately through personal experience, not through recorded biblical history and the mediation of memory. People don't want to remember what God has done in ages past; they want to feel his presence right now. Of course, experiencing God through his Spirit is one of life's greatest treasures. But we neglect the past to our peril. Subjective experience of God, however wonderful when it is genuine, must be interpreted in light of historic revelation. When people are cut off from salvation history, they are easily carried away from orthodox faith and from the real God. They end up creating their own images of God and worshiping the false image just like the Israelites did:

> They made a calf at Horeb
> > and worshiped a cast image.
> They exchanged the glory of God
> > for the image of an ox that eats grass.
> *They forgot God,* their Savior,
> > who had done great things in Egypt. (Psalm 106:19-21)

The Israelites fabricated a god that fit their cultural expectations. And so do we when we forget the God of history. We end up not with golden calves but with gods that reflect our own ethos. We worship gods of relativism, materialism, and emotionalism. Our gods wink at our sin rather than judging it and delivering us from it. They give us good feelings, at least momentarily, but ultimately leave us unsatisfied and tethered to nothing other than our own imagination.

Prayers of remembrance, however, keep us anchored to the Rock, to the real God who revealed himself in history. The more we recount in prayer what God has done, the more our relationship with him will be genuine, lasting, and growing. And, ironically, the more it will be emotionally satisfying.

We Will Be Refreshed in Our Relationship with the Living God

If you want to be refreshed in your relationship with God, don't focus on your desire so much as on the God who can fulfill it. What better way to focus on

God than to remember his wonderful works, both in biblical history and in your own life? Recollection in prayer leads not only to a genuine relationship with the real God but also to an ongoing renewal of that relationship.

It's like the renewal in my marriage. My love for Linda remains constant from day to day. But after twenty years of marriage, my feelings of love for her ebb and flow. It's hard for me to adore my dear wife each day with the same intensity I experienced on our wedding day. Now we both rush in opposite directions, driving our kids to innumerable activities, attending meetings, and simply trying to keep afloat as the tide of busyness rises all around us. Thank God for wedding anniversaries and other special occasions when I take time to stop and rekindle my love for Linda.

My anniversary tradition is quite simple. I don't sit and try to rev up feelings for my wife. Instead, I go on a walk in a secluded place where I can be alone with the Lord. As I walk I remember in prayer. I think of all the ways Linda has blessed me, and I share these with God. I ask him to remind me of things I've forgotten. As I do, my heart overflows with gratitude to the Lord and with new love for my wife. I remember that Linda is a gift from the gracious hand of God. Remembering leads to refreshment, both in human relationships and in our relationship with God.

Recollection of God's faithfulness in the past can be especially tender when we are feeling plowed under by sin or pummeled by suffering. The Psalms model remembering prayer in circumstances such as these. In Psalm 42, for example, the psalmist was thirsting for God, having cried day and night. So what did he do? He remembered: "My soul is cast down within me; therefore I remember you" (Psalm 42:6). His recollection of God's power and goodness led the psalmist to renewed trust in God's steadfast love and revived hope in divine help.

When you are spiritually dry and your soul thirsts for God, do you try to rev up some new feeling, or do you remember who God is and what he has done? Do you start sinking into the depths of your neediness, or do you consider the God who has met your needs in the past?

Today I heard a disheartening report about a ministry into which I've poured my heart. Finding out that things are not going well, I felt as if all my strength drained out of my soul. I wondered how, given my discouragement,

I could find the energy to write about prayer. My usual practice would be to lay my sadness before God in prayer, which I did, and to ask for his help, which I did. But it occurred to me that I had a chance to practice what I'm preaching in this chapter. So I spent time remembering in prayer how God had blessed the struggling ministry.

"Lord, you began this ministry in a wondrous way," I prayed. "It was so obviously a work of your hand. And you have guided it." I continued to pray like this for about five minutes. As I finished I felt a bit of relief from worry about the future of this particular ministry. But more important, I felt reassured about what matters most: that God is God, that God is good, and that he holds all things, including the ailing ministry, in his gracious hands.

Songwriter Matt Redman testifies to the renewing power of remembering in his stirring song "When My Heart Runs Dry":

> When my heart runs dry
> And there's no song to sing
> No holy melody
> No words of love within
> I recall the height from which
> This fragile heart has slipped…
>
> And I'll remember You
> I will turn back and do
> The things I used to do
> For the love of You.
> Lord, I'll remember You
> I will turn back and do
> The things I used to do
> For the love of You.[3]

We Will Know Our Place in God's World

Many of us don't know where we fit in the grand scheme of things. We have been uprooted from the places that once defined our existence. We leave behind our neighborhoods, hometowns, or homelands. A culture that prizes the here and now severs us from our past. We also lose touch with foundational stories that tell us who we are and what we're to do. A postmodern world filled with competing stories, none of which tells us definitively where we fit, casts us adrift from the past. Our culture has lost the one story that truly defines us and our world.

Prayers of remembrance help us know our place in the world. As we recollect what God has done in history, we discover where we belong. Like the Israelites, we have been chosen by God to be his special people. We are his stewards, saints, and servants. We belong to the Lord, not because of any virtue in ourselves, but because of his grace that has redeemed us and set us apart for his purposes. As we prayerfully remember God's works, we rehearse the drama in which we play a crucial role. We discover who we are, to whom we belong, and where we fit in the big picture.

If our remembering prayers are shared in Christian community, then we will establish not only our own place in God's world but also the place of the next generation. We will help our offspring know who they are and where they belong as children of their heavenly Father. Psalm 78 highlights the connection between remembering and instructing future generations:

> I will open my mouth in a parable;
>   I will utter dark sayings from old,
> things that we have heard and known,
>   that our ancestors have told us.
> We will not hide them from their children;
>   we will tell to the coming generation
> the glorious deeds of the LORD, and his might,
>   and the wonders that he has done.
>
> He established a decree in Jacob,
>   and appointed a law in Israel,
> which he commanded our ancestors
>   to teach to their children;
> that the next generation might know them,
>   the children yet unborn,

and rise up and tell them to their children,

 so that they should set their hope in God,

and not forget the works of God,

 but keep his commandments. (verses 2-7)

In a world of confusing and contradictory stories, our children need to know the one story that matters most. It's the true story of divine salvation. Through telling this story in prayer, both we and our children will find our place in God's world.

The power of remembering—and the pain of forgetting—are poignantly portrayed in the movie *Avalon*. As the film begins, we hear a voice saying, "I came to America in 1914…by way of Philadelphia…. That's where I got off the boat, and then I came to Baltimore. It was the most beautiful place you've ever seen in your life." As the movie progresses, we identify the voice as that of Sam, the patriarch of an immigrant family. He is recounting his own history, passing it along to his grandchildren. But many in the family are bored with the old stories. They'd rather live in the present and allow television to tell the story that shapes their lives.

As they abandon the past, however, the present betrays them. Family members lose touch with their identity. They break relationship with one another for trivial reasons. They no longer know who they are or where they belong.

When the movie concludes, Sam is living alone in a retirement home, where he is visited by his grandson Michael and his great-grandson, also named Sam. Old Sam continues to tell the same stories. The last words we hear him speak are those that began the movie: "I came to America in 1914…"

When Michael and his son leave the rest home, young Sam complains, "Dad, that man talks funny."

"He wasn't born here, Sam," Michael explains.

"You mean he wasn't born in Baltimore?" Sam asks.

"He came to America in 1914. He said it was the most beautiful place he's ever seen."

And so the movie ends, right where it began, but two generations removed.[4]

Unlike his other relatives who want to live only in the present, Michael understands the value of family history and his responsibility to pass it on to the next generation.

Similarly, the Psalms teach us to remember our family history as children of God. When we prayerfully recount what God has done, and when we do this with our children, both we and future generations will find our place in the ultimate story of God's grace.

This insight has impacted the way I pray with my own children. Ever since Nathan and Kara were infants, I have prayed with them every night when I tuck them into bed. I always begin by thanking God for the good things that have happened to them during the day. For example, I might pray, "Thank you, Jesus, that Kara could go to school today and learn. Thank you for how hard she works in school and for how much she loves her teacher and her friends. Please help her not to be discouraged when her schoolwork is hard."

But in light of the Psalms, I now pray with an expanded perspective. I acknowledge God's grace not only in the immediate experience of my children but also in biblical history. Then I connect that history to the personal experiences of my children. For example, I might pray, "Thank you, God, for loving us so much that you sent your Son to die on a cross for us. Even though we were sinners, you showed us your mercy. Lord, you have saved Kara because you love her. You have called her to be your disciple. Please help her to live for you every day of her life. And thank you that Kara could go to school today."

In small prayers that match my children's maturity level, I help them see themselves in light of the grand story of grace. We remember together the mighty works of God so that we might know who we are as God's people.

We Will Be Prepared for Worship

I will touch upon this fourth reward of remembrance only briefly because it will be developed more thoroughly later in this book. Put simply, remembering prepares us for worship.

One of the strongest calls to worship in the Psalms appears in Psalm 103. It begins,

Bless the LORD, O my soul,
   and all that is within me,
   bless his holy name.
Bless the LORD, O my soul,
   and do not forget all his benefits. (verses 1-2)

God will be blessed when we do not forget—or, to put it positively, when we do remember—his many benefits. And this is exactly what the rest of Psalm 103 does. It recounts God's forgiveness, healing, justice, revelation, heavenly rule, and so on.

When we gather for worship, we often find that we're not ready. Our hearts seem miles away from God. Our minds are distracted. Our bodies restless. What should we do? Some would suggest that we need to rev up our spiritual engines, to get some spiritual adrenaline pumping. Maybe we'll get some inspiration from a booming pipe organ or pounding drums. According to this theory, our job is to manufacture enthusiasm for God. But this approach, though it can appear to work for a season, is doomed to fail because genuine worship is not about our emotional state, but about God and his glory.

The Psalms offer another approach. If our hearts are unprepared for worship, we should turn our gaze not upon our own parched souls but upon God. We should remember his wonders and recall his mighty deeds. At times we'll also be reminded of our own failures, which will further accentuate God's glorious grace. Thus, prayer of remembering is a prelude to genuine worship, besides being one of its central features. Remembering what God has done undergirds our gratitude and intensifies our praise.

An Exercise in Prayer of Remembering

Read Psalm 105 carefully, prayerfully. As you do, allow God's Spirit to excite your heart through the recital of God's mighty works. You may find it helpful to read the psalm at least twice, once to get an overall sense, and a second time to linger upon words and phrases. When you have finished a prayerful reading of Psalm 105, continue to recount God's mighty works in prayer. Consider the ongoing work of God throughout Scripture, especially in Jesus Christ. Then, building upon this biblical foundation, remember God's saving work in your own life. Tell him how you have experienced his grace. Don't rush; allow the Spirit to refresh your memory—and your soul—in the process.

This exercise can be done privately, but it also can be adapted to a corporate setting. Let me encourage you to do it in the context of your family, with a prayer group or small-group Bible study, or in a church Sunday-school class.

In addition to Psalm 105, you may also do this exercise with Psalms 78 and 106. These will help you remember how God's grace has overcome even our rebellion against him.

Be still, and know that I am God!
    I am exalted among the nations,
    I am exalted in the earth.

      —Psalm 46:10

For God alone my soul waits in silence,
    for my hope is from him.
He alone is my rock and my salvation,
    my fortress; I shall not be shaken.
On God rests my deliverance and my honor;
    my mighty rock, my refuge is in God.

Trust in him at all times, O people;
    pour out your heart before him;
    God is a refuge for us.

      —Psalm 62:5-8

O Lord, my heart is not lifted up,
    my eyes are not raised too high;
I do not occupy myself with things
    too great and too marvelous for me.
But I have calmed and quieted my soul,
    like a weaned child with its mother;
    my soul is like the weaned child that is with me.

O Israel, hope in the Lord
    from this time on and forevermore.

      —Psalm 131:1-3

THE QUIET AFTER THE STORM

Prayer of Silence

E arly one morning I stumbled into Tully's Coffee, my favorite local hang-out. Nobody else was there, other than the young woman who served up a strong brew. As I sat sipping my coffee, I felt surprisingly quiet, as if my soul were drinking in the stillness of the morning. I wondered why I hadn't felt this way before at Tully's.

All of a sudden my quiet reverie was interrupted by a cry from the woman behind the counter. "Oh my gosh," she exclaimed, "I *completely* forgot to turn on the music. I'm so sorry." Before I could say anything to absolve her guilt, she scurried off into the back room. A few seconds later the predictably cheerful tones of soft rock filled the previously silent air. Only then did I realize why I had felt so peaceful. It was the result of a few hushed moments, a blessed interlude uninterrupted by the Backstreet Boys or Mariah Carey.

Trapped in a Noisy World

Have you ever stopped to listen to all the noises that flood our lives? Cell phones interrupt intimate conversations. Pagers pierce the stillness of sleep or the reverence of a memorial service. Intercoms, car warning systems, answering machines, and personal digital assistants summon our attention. Throw in the din produced by blaring car stereos, power lawn mowers, leaf blowers, sirens, televisions, Nintendo sets, and omnipresent Muzak, and you have the beginnings of a sonic nightmare. Of course, I haven't even mentioned the clamor of human voices, whether they belong to the man in the next booth who's chattering too loudly on his cell phone or to your kids who are hollering over who gets to use the computer.

We often feel so harassed by the noisiness of our lives that we yearn for silence—or at least we think we do. I often find myself wishing, *Oh, what I'd do for just a little bit of peace and quiet!* But if I got my wish, would I actually enjoy the quiet? Or would I instead do what I usually do when an oasis of silence presents itself? Most of the time I find a way to disturb the peace. I snap on the television or a CD player. I do chores. I phone a friend—anything but savor the silence I so deeply need. The world of my heart can seem as noisy as the world around me.

Our Need for Silence

I desperately need some genuine quiet in my life, and so do you. We need to escape not just from the acoustic din in which we live but from the psychic racket that scrambles our souls. We need to discover how to enjoy true, restful stillness. Wouldn't you like to follow the Lord's invitation: "Be still, and know that I am God!" (Psalm 46:10)? Don't you yearn to echo the confident confession of Psalm 131:

> But I have calmed and quieted my soul,
>> like a weaned child with its mother;
>> my soul is like the weaned child that is with me. (verse 2)

Why do we need such quiet moments? It is often said, truly, that quiet is prerequisite to hearing God. How can we expect to receive divine guidance if we have filled our ears and our hearts with distractions? Since the Lord speaks to us, as he once did to Elijah, in "a still small voice" (1 Kings 19:12, KJV), we'll miss his whisper unless our hearts are quiet.[1]

To be sure, silence helps us live God-directed lives. But the Psalms don't emphasize this result of quietness. Rather, they present silence more as the gracious end of a process rather than a means to some other worthy end, such as hearing God's whisper. Silence is a way of being with God, a relational dynamic in which we actually "enjoy God," to use the language of the West-minster Shorter Catechism.[2] It's living in calm peace and quiet trust, free from worry or pride. Why would any of us avoid this?

The Way to Silence

Given the noisiness in our world and our own hearts, how can we be silent? How can we join David in his confident prayer: "For God alone my soul waits in silence" (Psalm 62:5)?

David penned Psalm 62 when he was being verbally battered by his ene-mies, who sought to knock him over like a "tottering fence" (see verse 3). Nev-ertheless, twice he said that his soul waited *"in silence"* for God (see verses 1,5). What gave David such assurance that he could be still in the midst of strident accusations? He explained the cause of his peacefulness this way:

> For God alone my soul waits in silence,
> 	for my hope is from him.
> He alone is my rock and my salvation,
> 	my fortress; I shall not be shaken. (verses 5-6)

David's silence is a direct result of his knowledge of God. God is rock solid and therefore trustworthy. God was David's salvation, the One who would rescue him yet again. God was his fortress, the place of ultimate safety.

Because David knew God and had a vital relationship with him, he could wait quietly even in the midst of the storm. The Hebrew rendering of verse 5 reads literally, "Only in God is my soul silent." *Only* in God! True quietness comes when we place our trust—indeed, our very lives—in God's hands alone.

In Psalm 62 David rejected other influences that compete for our trust. Verses 9 and 10 warn us against relying upon that which sometimes seems so trustworthy: people and money. When people lose their jobs, for example, often their first thought is, *Well, at least I have lots of contacts, not to mention my friends and family.* Or they might think, *At least we've saved up some money for a time like this.* It's natural to put our trust in things other than God, but it's ultimately disappointing. As David reminds us, anything we rely upon apart from God will ultimately let us down. Friends move away. Family members die. Savings accounts dwindle. The Dow Jones Average plummets. But God is always there, always our Rock, Salvation, and Fortress.

When we know God in this way, our hearts can be truly at rest. Then we can be silent as we wait upon God, even when his timetable is not our own. This kind of silence flows not from exhaustion or resignation but from confidence and certain hope in God alone.

THE STORM BEFORE THE CALM

There is a danger in what I have just said. It's the danger of forcing your soul into premature or pretended silence.

You may feel as if you're in the valley of the shadow of death right now. Fear, discouragement, and despair have taken up residence in your soul. But then I talk about trusting God and being silent. After reading Psalm 62:5, "For God alone my soul waits in silence," you conclude you'd better just be quiet and act as if you trust God, even though your heart wants to cry out for God's help. I have heard Christians rebuke others for praying too much about some problem. "You should trust God more," they say. "You need to stop praying so much and have more faith." This is a call for premature silence, or even pretending.

Shouting out to God for help, even repeatedly, is not a sign of lack of faith. Just the opposite: It's a sign that we trust God to help us. He urges us to ask in every time of need and for every type of need. We must hold the Scripture's teaching on silence in creative tension with the Psalms' teachings on other forms of prayer. Prayers of silence must go hand in hand with asking, praise, and even shouting.

Whenever we take a Bible verse out of context, we inevitably misinterpret it. This is certainly true for Psalm 62:5. David did indeed wait quietly for God, but this didn't erase his freedom to tell the Lord everything that was on his heart. Notice carefully what he says only three verses later about our interaction with God: "Trust in him at all times, O people; *pour out your heart before him;* God is a refuge for us" (verse 8). How startling! A few lines earlier David spoke of waiting in silence. Then, sandwiched in between the command to trust in God and the affirmation that God is our refuge, we find "pour out your heart before him." Wouldn't you expect something like "quiet your heart before him"? After all, the fact that we can trust God to be our refuge is what enables us to be quiet. Yet in this verse David encourages us to pour out to God everything in our hearts. Don't hide your worries and fears! Don't clean up your prayers! Don't pretend to be peacefully silent when your heart is raging! Rather, freely lay before God everything you think and feel— and keep on doing so until you've poured it all out. Only then will your silence be genuine.

If what I've just said sounds suspiciously like pop psychobabble, read carefully the comment on Psalm 62:8 by sixteenth-century theologian John Calvin, a man who was clearly not a victim of the hypertherapeutic spirit of our age:

> As we are all too apt [in difficult times] to shut up our affliction in our own breast—a circumstance which can only aggravate the trouble and imbitter the mind against God, David could not have suggested a better expedient than that of disburdening our cares to him, and thus, as it were, pouring out our hearts before him.... What the Psalmist advises is all the more necessary, considering the mischievous tendency which we have naturally to keep our troubles pent up in our breasts till they drive us to despair. Usually, indeed, men show much anxiety and ingenuity in seeking to escape from the troubles which may happen to press upon them; but so long as they shun coming into the presence of God, they only involve themselves in a labyrinth of difficulties. Not to insist farther upon the words, David is here to be considered as exposing that diseased but deeply-rooted principle in our nature, which leads us to hide our griefs, and ruminate upon them, instead of relieving ourselves at once by pouring out our prayers and complaints before God.[3]

Writing more than four hundred years ago, Calvin spoke as if he knew our hearts today. He knew that the silence commended in Psalm 62 must not hold us back from pouring out our hearts to God. On the contrary, the silence of this psalm comes as a direct result of just such openness before God.

Because David has held nothing back from the Lord, he has once again experienced God's solidness, and therefore he can be silent.

The calm of God usually comes not before the storm or instead of the storm but after the storm. After the torrent of our prayer, God gives us his miraculous peace "which surpasses all understanding" (Philippians 4:7).

CHILDLIKE QUIET IN THE LAP OF GOD

Young children are especially good at pouring out their hearts. If they're happy, they gush with pleasure. If they're sad, tears flow unreservedly. And if they're angry, watch out! Even the best kids indulge in periodic tantrums.

For this reason I find David's simile in Psalm 131 surprising:

> But I have calmed and quieted my soul,
>> like a weaned child with its mother;
>> my soul is like the weaned child that is with me. (verse 2)

A "weaned child" was someone of preschool age, around three or four years old. How many calm, quiet preschoolers do you know? I think of them as the epitome of activity, not peacefulness.

But there are times when children this age do quiet down, and David must have envisioned such a time. It's a time when a child is resting upon a mother's lap, being held and comforted. David presented a picture of the calm that comes after the storm, the stillness that follows the tantrum or the noisy celebration.

In Psalm 62 David was silent because God is big and strong, a rock and a fortress. In Psalm 131 David was quiet because God is like a comforting mother. The psalmist had experienced personally what God promised the Israelites through the prophet Isaiah: "As a mother comforts her child, so I will comfort you" (Isaiah 66:13). The awesome King of kings who rules the universe, the solid Rock that cannot be moved, this God reaches out to us with a mother's tenderness, soothing our fears and quieting our hearts.

When I suffered from nightmares as a child, I'd call for my parents and they'd come running to comfort me. I can still remember the secure feeling of being held by my mother as she rocked me back to sleep, singing softly to chase away my bad dreams. I was, literally, a weaned child with his mother, calmed and quieted.

Psalm 131 further resolves the apparent tension in Psalm 62, the tension between silence and pouring out our hearts to God. At times in our relationship with God, we will, like children, cry out to him in pain or even scream in anger. Yet, as the outpouring draws us near to God, he reaches out to us, embracing us like a mother with her child. In the arms of the Lord, we find his peace and, with peace, the gift of silence.

Sharing Silence Together

Psalm 131 presents yet another surprise, in addition to the unexpected image of a quiet preschooler. The first two verses of this psalm are some of the most personal in all of the Psalter. Here David professed humble trust in the Lord, comparing himself to a little child with its mother. But then he shared this intimate moment with the whole nation: "O Israel, hope in the LORD from this time on and forevermore" (verse 3). David's relationship with God was deeply personal, but not private. He shared his experience of God's tenderness so that others might enjoy humble quietness before God.

Psalm 131 teaches us to regard silent prayer as something both private and corporate. It is something to be experienced when we are alone with God and when we are gathered together as God's people. We need to be silent in our prayer closets and in our worship centers, in our private devotions and in our public gatherings.

What I've just said about silence in corporate worship might strike you as odd. Throughout the Christian world we enjoy celebrative, exuberant worship. Praise God! But along the way we've lost touch with the reverent awe of shared silence.

Three years ago I took a twelve-week sabbatical from my work as a pastor. During this time my wife and I worshiped in a variety of churches throughout Southern California. In every church the worship was vibrant, God-honoring, and gloriously noisy. But it seemed that silence had been excommunicated. Every spare second of the worship experience was filled with sound.

This description can fit my own church as well, though we do try to include at least a few moments of intentional silence in each of our services. Sometimes, however, unplanned silence has brought unplanned blessings. Several years ago a young woman in my church sang "How Great Thou Art" as an offertory solo. Julie's stunning soprano voice lifted our spirits as she proclaimed God's greatness in song. But as she came to the third verse, her voice began to waver. Singing about the wonder of Christ's sacrifice, Julie choked up. The meaning of what she was singing overwhelmed her, and she struggled to continue. By the final verse and chorus, Julie just stood there in silence before us, offering herself to God.

I can't remember a more moving moment in a worship service. Everyone in the congregation was caught up before God, not only because of Julie's exceptional singing, but especially because of her exceptional silence. When the pianist finished playing, nobody said a word for several seconds as we joined Julie in silent worship. For those precious moments we were still, and we knew that the Lord was God.

From Buzzing to Being

If you wish to grow in your experience of prayerful silence, let me recommend that you set aside an extended period of time for silence. It might be an hour or a half day or even longer. If your life is as busy as mine, you'll need to plan for this well in advance. But the effort will pay off bountifully.

I must warn you, however, that if you're unused to being quiet before God, you'll probably find the experience confusing, even frustrating at first. My first try at a silent retreat began as a total disaster.

Several years ago my wife and I, along with some Christian friends, planned to spend a weekend in silence. When we arrived at the secluded retreat center on Friday evening, our bedroom was stifling because the temperature had climbed into the nineties during the day, and the window of our room had been shut. Cranking it open for ventilation, we left for the beginning of the retreat. The leader explained the importance of keeping silent for two days and warned us that it might be difficult at first. He had no idea how prophetic his words would be for me!

When Linda and I returned to our room at bedtime, the temperature had dropped considerably, and instead, we found about a hundred ravenous mosquitoes. The window of our room did not have a screen. Without talking, Linda and I quietly divided our efforts at bug swatting until most of the obnoxious little vampires had perished. In the process I received a dozen bites.

For most people mosquito bites are an inconvenience, but for me they're a nightmare because I'm allergic to bug bites. Soon my body was covered with quarter-size welts that itched worse than anything I could remember. For hours I sat in agonizing silence, trying not to scratch my bites because I knew that would only make my allergic reaction worse. I spent most of that night peering sleeplessly into the darkness, trying to maintain my sanity. I wanted to break the silence by shouting out, "I'm itching to death! I can't stand it!"

At about five in the morning, Linda awoke. Out of pity she broke her silence to see how I was feeling.

"Are you okay?" she asked softly. "Is there anything I can do for you?"

"No, I'm not okay," I said. "I'm itching like mad. I haven't slept one wink. And I can't even complain because of this crazy silence! But, no, there's nothing you can do for me."

Finally, exhaustion overcame my itching, and as the sun started to rise, I feel asleep. By late morning I had recovered enough to take a walk in the woods, with my body bathed in insect repellent. Finding a tranquil spot by a stream, I sat down to be quiet before God. Yet as I tried to be silent, I still heard a hundred buzzing mosquitoes—not real ones this time, but the "mosquitoes" that were living inside my head. Droning inside me were the demands, needs, ideas, hopes, fears, memories, disappointments, and dreams that filled and often controlled my life. And these bugs couldn't be swatted. As I sat by the stream and surrendered to God everything that entered my mind, slowly I sensed my soul beginning to simmer down.

During the last day of the retreat, I relished the silence that enveloped me. I was consistently in touch with the Lord but didn't feel the need to fill our encounter with my words. I could take time to reflect upon God's Word, not so much with harried analysis as with an open heart. By the end of the retreat, I was like a weaned child in its mother's lap, quiet and secure. Although I had begun the weekend with trepidation, wondering how in the world I'd make it for two days without talking, by the end I didn't want to stop being quiet.

I began to discover why so many spiritually mature Christians set aside regular times for extended silence and solitude. These grace-filled disciplines help us quiet our hearts so we can hear the whisper of the Spirit. More important, they help us experience being with God rather than just doing for God. Of course, living for God each day is essential to faithful discipleship. But it's so easy for us to turn the Christian life into an endless series of good deeds rather than an intimate relationship with the living God, who gives meaning to our deeds. Silence before God helps quiet the buzzing distractions of life so we can focus on being with the One who is the Way, the Truth, and Life.

Entering the Rest of Jesus

By God's grace and the encouragement of my fellow Christians, I have begun to discover the joy of silent prayer. But I don't claim any mastery in this area. By nature and by training, I am a person of words. Words aren't bad, of course. In fact, they're a primary means by which God makes his eternal Word known to us. But I'll freely confess that I can fill my heart with so many words that I leave little space for the Word of God. How often I forget the insight of Ecclesiastes: "For dreams come with many cares, and a fool's voice with many words" (5:3). Even more pointedly, sometimes my prayers are so filled with my words that God can't get a word in edgewise. How I need to remember the wisdom of Jesus:

> When you are praying, do not heap up empty phrases as the Gentiles
> do; for they think that they will be heard because of their many words.
> Do not be like them, for your Father knows what you need before you
> ask him. (Matthew 6:7-8)

In spite of my innate verbosity, I have begun to enjoy the refreshment of silence before God. I'm not speaking here merely of physical silence or of simply being quiet, but of being *quiet with God.* Sometimes this happens when I am with other believers sharing silence together. Sometimes it happens when I'm alone with the Lord. Sometimes it happens when I'm enjoying fellowship with others. But no matter the setting, I let myself lie back against the reassuring strength of God, like a child rocking in the lap of its mother. I put down the heavy burdens of my self-reliance, my compulsive need to understand or control. In these quiet moments I remain still while I simply allow God to be God.

Listen to Jesus's invitation to you:

> Come to me, all you that are weary and are carrying heavy burdens, and
> I will give you rest. Take my yoke upon you, and learn from me; for I
> am gentle and humble in heart, and you will find rest for your souls.
> For my yoke is easy, and my burden is light. (Matthew 11:28-30)

Will you accept the rest for your soul that Jesus offers? Will you put down your many words, your restless strivings, your heavy burdens, and rest quietly in him?

Listen to God's invitation to you: "Be still, and know that I am God!" (Psalm 46:10). Will you be still and let God be God?

An Exercise in Prayer of Silence

Use Psalms 46, 62, and 131 to guide you into silence before God. If this is to happen effectively, you need to be in a place of quiet, away from blaring televisions or invasive phone calls. Perhaps you can go to a nearby retreat center, or to your church's sanctuary during weekday hours, or to a secluded park. As you attempt to be quiet, be prepared for the thoughts and feelings that will buzz in your head and heart. Don't fret about them, but simply give them to God. Let the invitation of Psalm 46:10 fill your heart: "Be still, and know that I am God!" Don't rush your time of stillness or feel disappointed if you don't have some sort of profound experience. Just savor whatever silence you experience.

It's often hard to be truly silent when we are alone. If you can find a way to share in silence with others, take advantage of this opportunity. Discuss the possibility with a couple of brothers or sisters in Christ, or maybe with your pastor. The company and accountability of shared silence will help quiet your soul.

Clap your hands, all you peoples;
    shout to God with loud songs of joy.
For the LORD, the Most High, is awesome,
    a great king over all the earth.
He subdued peoples under us,
    and nations under our feet.
He chose our heritage for us,
    the pride of Jacob whom he loves.

God has gone up with a shout,
    the LORD with the sound of a trumpet.
Sing praises to God, sing praises;
    sing praises to our King, sing praises.
For God is the king of all the earth;
    sing praises with a psalm.

God is king over the nations;
    God sits on his holy throne.
The princes of the peoples gather
    as the people of the God of Abraham.
For the shields of the earth belong to God;
    he is highly exalted.

    —PSALM 47:1-9

A STANDING OVATION
FOR GOD

Prayer of Physical Expression

T he LORD is in his holy temple; let all the earth keep silence before him!"[1] So intoned Mrs. Merrill solemnly as she called the first-grade department of Hollywood Presbyterian Church to worship. Every week it was the same: "The LORD is in his holy temple; let all the earth keep silence before him."

And so we did, more or less. Even though we were wiggly first graders, we knew we were in a place of quiet reverence, a place where noisiness was inappropriate if not blasphemous. At the young age of seven, we were learning to worship in good Presbyterian fashion: decently, in order, and, above all, *quietly*. We sat up straight. We listened attentively. At times we sang joyfully, but never too boisterously. That simply wasn't the right way to worship.

All of this suited me just fine. By nature and background I'm not terribly expressive. Though I feel things deeply, I tend to keep my emotions inside. I don't even cheer loudly at ball games. Consequently, reverence before God, which in my growing-up years meant quietness, came easily to me.

So you can imagine the shock to my system when, as a junior in college, I worshiped one Sunday morning with an African American Pentecostal congregation. Some friends and I had gone on retreat to a church in Bridgeport, Connecticut. Though the members of our host church were Anglos, they had a close partnership with Deliverance Tabernacle, an African American congregation in the same town. So several of us decided to worship with the folks at Deliverance, figuring that a cross-cultural experience would stretch us a bit.

A bit? That worship service stretched me far beyond anything I could have imagined. For one thing, the service began at 9:30 and lasted until well past noon. A three-hour service was more than twice what I had ever experienced before.

You might imagine that I became bored during such a long service, but nothing could be further from the truth. Throughout those three hours, I felt uncomfortable, awkward, nervous, fascinated, and inspired, but not bored. I don't think anyone who worshiped at Deliverance Tabernacle ever felt bored. Excited? Yes. Joyful? You bet. Pumped up? Always. But bored? Never!

The sisters and brothers in this church also seemed never to have heard Mrs. Merrill's line about keeping silent before God. They praised God thunderously, with pounding drums and a rollicking Hammond organ. Their gospel-style singing was more like shouting than anything I'd ever heard in church before. They stood, clapped, lifted their hands, rocked back and forth, and even danced as they sang. At one point the pastor urged us to praise the Lord by skipping around the sanctuary. Never in my life had I felt more stiff, gawky, and painfully Anglo. Mountains may be able to skip like rams in the presence of God (see Psalm 114:4), but not me. To this day I'm thankful that the pastor didn't try to get me to dance in worship. After seeing me skip, I think he realized that would have been more of an abomination than an edifying act of worship.

Since that morning at Deliverance Tabernacle, I've learned to be more expressive in worship, to a point. No skipping, please, but I'm now far more open in expressing praise to our Lord. And I haven't been alone in my journey. During the last two decades, many Christians have learned to communicate their praise physically, by vigorous singing, lifting hands, or clapping. Liturgical dance has enlivened the traditional sedateness of many churches. Congregations that once majored in solemnity now feature so-called contemporary services, with rock bands amplified to raise the dead. Churches that formerly avoided physical celebration now delight in it.

Yet there are still many God-loving Christians who aren't so sure about physical exertion in worship. Whatever happened to keeping silence before God? After all, Mrs. Merrill didn't make up that line. She took it straight out of the Bible (see Habakkuk 2:20). Does God's command in Psalm 46:10— "Be still, and know that I am God!"—no longer apply to Christian worship? Furthermore, what if we just aren't comfortable expressing ourselves physically as we worship? If my personal comfort level or my culture prefers sedentary worship, is this okay? Is there any reason why I should stretch beyond what comes easily for me?

With these questions in mind, let's turn again to the Psalms, where we'll find answers that will help us worship God more completely. We'll discover the role of physical prayer in our relationship with God and see how it can enrich our communication with him. (You'll notice that I speak about physical worship and physical prayer as if they are virtually synonymous. Worship is a form of prayer in which we communicate our praise, love, and submission to God.)

THE NEED FOR ENERGETIC EXPRESSION

More than one hundred times the Psalms tell us to do something with our bodies as we pray.[2] Consider Psalm 47:

> Clap your hands, all you peoples;
> > shout to God with loud songs of joy....
> Sing praises to God, sing praises;
> > sing praises to our King, sing praises.
> For God is the king of all the earth;
> > sing praises with a psalm. (verses 1,6-7)

Do you get the idea that the psalmist wants us to use our bodies as we praise God?

Elsewhere in the Psalms we're told not just to sing but to do so "with loud shouts" (33:3). In many passages we're instructed to use our bodies in worship, whether by standing in awe or kneeling in reverence or lifting our hands in blessing (see Psalms 22:23; 95:6; and 134:2). And, just for the record, the Psalms *never* encourage us to sit in worship. God alone sits upon his throne as we assume the postures of servanthood, either standing or bowing before him.

The Psalms illustrate the value of energetic physical expression in prayer. Of course, you may be perfectly comfortable with all of this, especially if your Christian community encourages physical movement in worship. But even active worshipers usually limit their modes of expression. Recently I was teaching a class at the Southern California Worship Institute. I asked worship leaders from churches across the country to raise their hands if people in their congregations regularly stood during worship. One hundred percent raised their hands. Then I asked about lifting hands during worship. About 75 percent answered affirmatively. Then I asked about kneeling in worship. No hands were raised. Of course, this result reflects the constituency of the class. Had I asked a room full of Episcopalian worship leaders, the proportions might have been reversed. It's rare to find a church that encourages a full range of physical expression in worship.

My purpose is not to measure the authenticity of your communication with God by tabulating the variety of physical expressions you employ during worship. Nor am I criticizing the worship practices of any church. I simply want you to realize that there are additional biblical modes of prayer for you to experience. Sometimes the holds we bar with God are the ones that involve our bodies. Sit quietly in prayer? Sure thing. Stand with arms upraised? No way!

If you're already comfortable with using your body in prayer, perhaps I can offer some deeper insight into its purpose. Our goal is to grow in our relationship with God. Standing, singing, shouting, clapping, kneeling, and the other actions of prayer are simply different means of communicating with the living God. Thus, we ought to utilize them for the sake of God's glory and our enjoyment of him.

Why Pray Through Physical Expressions?

But, you may ask, are physical expressions of prayer really that important? For me, worshipful hands are folded hands, not raised hands. And shouting, clapping, kneeling—well, these just give me the willies. Why do we have to do these things?

Let me say clearly that engaging in the full range of postures and physical movements in prayer is *not* necessary for everyone. Though the Psalms call us to lots of physical activity in prayer, some deeply spiritual people simply can't participate. In my church, for example, we have a number of senior adults who have difficulty standing. They'd love to stand before God as a gesture of reverence, but physically they aren't able to do so. Moreover, I know Christians who are paralyzed from the neck down. What they can do with their bodies is quite limited, but their worship is not. They give God all that they are, even though their movements are restricted. What matters most in our communication with God is what's in our hearts, not the words we speak or the gestures we make.

But if we are blessed with bodies that can be employed in prayer, we should use the full range of postures and movements that are taught in Scripture. I would suggest two main reasons for this: the first has to do with the nature of God and the second has to do with our own nature.

Responding to the Kingly Greatness of God

Psalm 47 begins by calling us to clap and shout to God. Then it provides the reason:

> Clap your hands, all you peoples;
>> shout to God with loud songs of joy.
> *For the LORD, the Most High, is awesome,*
>> *a great king over all the earth.* (verses 1-2)

Similarly, this psalm urges an abundance of singing for essentially the same reason:

> Sing praises to God, sing praises;
>> sing praises to our King, sing praises.
> *For God is the king of all the earth;*
>> sing praises with a psalm. (verses 6-7)

The greatness, majesty, and sovereignty of God call forth excessive praise. His unique and glorious nature impels us to clap, shout, and sing praises.

These expressions make sense in light of Israel's experience of human kingship. Consider, for example, the coronation of Joash. During the ninth century BC, the Israelites suffered under the debauched, brutal rule of tyrants. In Judah, Queen Athaliah murdered most of her own relatives to guarantee her longevity as ruler. But her infant grandson, Joash, was secretly rescued and hidden in the temple for the six long years of Athaliah's reign. When Joash was only seven years old, the priest and his co-conspirators crowned the boy king. After doing so, "they *clapped their hands and shouted*, 'Long live the king!'" (2 Kings 11:12). Merely thinking *Long live the king!* wouldn't have been enough. Nor would whispering have been. A moment like this demanded clapping and shouting—nothing less. The coronation of Joash called forth noisy celebration.

Psalm 47 envisions the coronation of God. He "has gone up with a shout, the LORD with the sound of a trumpet" (verse 5). "Gone up"? To where? To sit upon his "holy throne" as "the princes of the peoples gather" to offer homage to the "great king over all the earth" (verses 2,8,9). Thus, loud celebration is fitting. The greatest king of all deserves this much and far more besides (see verse 2).

Since we know God to be not only our Sovereign but the King of kings, surely we ought to celebrate his sovereignty with clapping, shouting, and singing. "But," one might object, "those expressions were appropriate in the ninth century BC. Things are different today." Are they? The last time I watched election results on television, every newly elected leader received riotous applause from his or her supporters. Acceptance speeches were continually interrupted by clapping, shouting, and general mayhem. Surely we don't believe that such expressions are good enough for governors and presidents, but not for the Lord!

In fact, we clap and shout for all sorts of luminaries, for athletes and rock stars, for victorious generals and Academy Award–winning actors. When you consider the all-surpassing superiority of God compared to all of these, don't you think the Lord deserves our applause? Maybe even a standing ovation that never ends? Maybe more?

Responding as Whole People

The nature of God calls forth all-encompassing expressions of praise. God deserves not just what our minds think or our hearts feel but everything we have to offer. And it's only when we offer everything that we worship God as whole people.

God created us as unified beings. In biblical perspective, we are not ethereal spirits housed within insignificant bodies, but integrated beings composed of spirit and body, heart and flesh.³ Therefore, Scripture calls us to love God not only with our "inside parts" but with our "outside parts" as well. As Jesus said, quoting God's classic summons to Israel, "You shall love the Lord your God with all your heart, and with all your soul, and with all your mind, and with all your strength" (Mark 12:30). In this same vein, the apostle Paul urges us "to present [our] bodies as a living sacrifice, holy and acceptable to God, which is your spiritual worship" (Romans 12:1). We cannot offer all that we are to God if we hold back parts of ourselves. The God who made us as whole people deserves our whole worship.

If, like me, you're not a physically expressive person by nature, this can sound like one more "should" to tack on to the list of Christian duties. But God doesn't just require our full expression, he also offers us the delightful *freedom* of full expression. Our heavenly Father seeks childlike communication from us. In return, we get to experience the joy of childlikeness.

My daughter, Kara, is amazingly free with her body, especially when you consider that she got half of her genes from me! For example, if I sit down to play a song on the piano, Kara races into the living room and starts dancing, floating freely in response to the music. Or if she is singing in a church choir, she has a hard time standing still because her body wants to move with the music.

Kara is at liberty to express herself with all that she is. She exemplifies a wholeness that, frankly, I envy. I don't particularly want to dance around my living room, but I would like to be free to praise the Lord without hesitation, without worrying about what others think of me. I want to know, love, worship, and pray to God as a whole person—just the way he created me in Christ (see Ephesians 2:10). I was created to give him all that I am. And so were you.

Yet if we feel hesitant, if we find loving God with our mind or heart easier than loving him with our strength, what should we do?

OVERCOMING OUR HESITATION

Most Christians I know feel at least *some* hesitation about *some* prayerful activities. They may be fine with loud singing but uncomfortable with shouting. They may love clapping their hands but not lifting their hands into the air. They may endorse standing but not kneeling.

One reason for our hesitation is simple human nature. People tend to be uncomfortable with novelty. We prefer doing what's familiar. When we're asked to do something new, we get queasy, maybe even resistant. This is especially true when it comes to something as personal as using our bodies in worship.

I learned this the hard way when I was director of college ministries at Hollywood Presbyterian Church. During the mid-1980s I became fascinated by biblical teaching on using our bodies in worship. For several weeks my Sunday-morning teaching of the college group focused on this issue. I'd search the Scriptures to see what I could learn about a particular mode of physical expression and then share it with the collegians. After teaching for a while, I'd lead the group in an experiment so we could put into practice what we had learned. The experiment with standing was a hit, as were our explorations of clapping and kneeling. *This group is really willing to try new things,* I thought.

But then I hit a wall of resistance. One Sunday morning I taught on lifting hands in prayer and then suggested that my students sing some praise songs and lift their hands to the Lord. Some of the collegians participated gladly. But others sang not only with their hands down but with their arms riveted to their sides and scowls on their faces. After the worship time concluded, I heard complaints such as I had never before heard. Students accused me of being manipulative, insensitive, and theologically suspect. One of my adult leaders charged me with trying to turn the college group into a Pentecostal church. From my point of view, all I had done was teach on a few biblical passages and suggest that we do what they said. But from the response to my teaching, you'd have thought I was imposing animal sacrifice.

As I spent many hours listening to my disgruntled students, I repeatedly heard them voice their discomfort with trying something that was completely unfamiliar. "We like to worship how we worship," they said in so many words. I later understood that they weren't just dyed-in-the-wool Presbyterians. Rather, they were dyed-in-the-wool human beings. Humans don't typically embrace change, at least not immediately. And humans harbor many fears. I heard my students voice fears of the unknown, fears of looking foolish, and fears that one episode of hand lifting had launched our college group down the slippery slope of emotionalism.

From one of my students I heard something that amused me. "I'm just not comfortable with lots of bodily expression," he said. "That's not who I am." I would have believed this young man except that I had seen him at a football game. There he was magically transformed into a cheering, yelling, clapping maniac. He hardly sat down the whole game. In truth, he was very comfortable expressing emotions with his body—but not in church.

If you find it uncomfortable to use your body in prayer, let me encourage you to be honest, both with yourself and with God. Tell the Lord you want to worship him with all that you are but simply aren't comfortable doing so. Ask for God's help. Ask for new freedom. Ask the Lord to guide you into those expressions that will be honoring to him and transforming for you.

God answers prayers like these. In fact, I watched the stiffest worshiper in the world become, by grace, one who was completely unreserved in worship. Throughout my childhood my dad was arguably the most unexpressive worshiper on the planet. It was painful to watch him. Because he believed he couldn't sing well, my dad didn't even try. During hymn singing he'd just stand there looking awkward and angry. He would never have been one to lift his hands or shout, even if our church had encouraged such things. My dad loved the Lord and served him faithfully. But that love never translated into expressive worship.

Then my dad got cancer. Surgery and chemotherapy forestalled the sorry conclusion to his illness, but my dad wanted to be healed completely, not just temporarily. So he did something out of character and attended a series of meetings led by a man known in Christian circles to be an instrument of divine healing. I tagged along.

The worship in these meetings was led by an excellent band that played nothing but contemporary praise songs. I knew my dad wouldn't like these songs, but then he didn't seem to like *any* church music. During the praise time at the first meeting, he sat stoically while I tried not to worry about how uncomfortable he must have been feeling. But during the second or third meeting, something strange began to happen. My dad started singing, softly and awkwardly at first, then louder and more energetically. By the last meeting he was actually lifting his hands to the Lord. My dad! Unbelievable, but true.

God didn't heal my dad's cancer, but he did heal his heart. From that time on, my dad experienced freedom and joy in worship that never ceased to amaze me. One of my favorite images of my dad comes from a worship service that happened during the last years of his life. He was standing up even though most of the congregation was seated. He was singing a praise song based on Psalm 97: "I exalt Thee, I exalt Thee, I exalt Thee, O Lord."[4] He was belting out this song, unconcerned about the quality of his singing voice. His hands weren't just lifted, they were soaring above his head like helium balloons. My dad was free, utterly free before God.

I want this kind of freedom for myself, and I want it for you, too. I'm not suggesting that physical expression is the only key to such liberty, as if you need merely to force your hands up, and your heart will open more completely to God. But from my own experience, I know that sometimes my heart remains closed until I offer to God the very thing that is holding me back from him—such as my discomfort over bodily movement during worship or my pride that makes me insist on doing things my way.

I'm still not always comfortable with the physical actions we associate with worship. It may never feel "natural" to me to lift my hands or kneel in worship. But I have told the Lord that I will give him everything he deserves from me. "If it's in the Bible," I pray, "then I'll do it." But I also ask for the inner freedom that only the Lord can give. Sometimes when I pray I picture my dad in the last years of his life as he worshiped with abandon: "Lord, make me like my dad! Give me the same freedom you gave him. Help me rejoice in you as he rejoiced, utterly free and utterly committed to you. O Lord, I want to worship you like that!"

A WORD OF CAUTION

I believe that physical expression in prayer, especially worship, matters. You've probably figured that out by now! But it doesn't matter nearly as much as some people think. In fact, some Christians are so obsessed with bodily movement that they miss what matters most in worship.

A friend of mine who leads worship in his church obsessively notes the number of hands raised while he's leading. If lots of hands go up, he's happy. If not, he concludes that worship wasn't "dynamic." He reminds me a little of the political pundits on television after the president's State of the Union speech. "That was an effective speech," they conclude, "because the president was interrupted *fifty-seven times* by applause." I can just hear my friend thinking, *Worship was great today because* fifty-seven *people raised their hands in praise.*

Let me offer a word of caution: *Don't confuse physical expression in prayer with the genuine item.* Yes, the Psalms teach us to pray by clapping, shouting, singing, and so forth. But just because we're doing these things doesn't mean we're truly communicating with God. It all depends on the heart.

Furthermore, if we follow the biblical example, certain gestures of prayer don't indicate spiritual zeal so much as spiritual need. My worship-leading friend, like many Christians today, mistakenly assumes that people lift their hands only when they are enraptured in worship. But the Psalms teach us to lift our hands not only in praise but also in desperation. "Hear the voice of my supplication," David prayed, "as I cry to you for help, as I lift up my hands toward your most holy sanctuary." (Psalm 28:2). Another psalmist prayed similarly:

You have caused my companions to shun me;
>   you have made me a thing of horror to them.
I am shut in so that I cannot escape;
>   my eye grows dim through sorrow.
Every day I call on you, O LORD;
>   I spread out my hands to you. (Psalm 88:8-9)

In this case, raised hands could hardly be counted as evidence of ecstatic worship. Following the biblical example, sometimes I spread out my hands in worship not because I'm flowing with praise but precisely because I'm not. I lift my hands in a gesture of neediness to the One who alone can inspire my praise.

Sometimes churches fall into a rut when it comes to expressions in worship. One Sunday morning during my tenure at Hollywood Presbyterian Church, the choir sang a stunning anthem. This music transported the congregation into the throne room of heaven. At the end of the anthem, we erupted in spontaneous applause, quite unusual at that time of the church's life. But for weeks thereafter the congregation clapped following every anthem, even if the piece itself suggested a quiet, reverential response. Clapping became an empty obligation rather than an act of genuine worship.

Psalm 47 calls us to clap our hands and "shout to God with loud songs of joy" (verse 1). But once again we must guard against assuming that loud singing should be the norm or that we can measure spiritual integrity by decibels. Sometimes the most powerful worship is quiet, even silent.

So, although I'm encouraging you to explore new avenues of physical prayer, remember that God looks upon the heart. What matters most isn't what you say or do or sing or shout, it's that you offer your *whole self* to God— and hold nothing back.

Offering All That We Are to God

I remember vividly the first time I ever offered all that I was to God in praise. It happened when I was about ten years old. My parents took me to a Sunday-evening church service to hear a woman named Gert Behanna share her testimony. What a testimony it was! Gert, though born into a privileged family, had lived dismally, experiencing three failed marriages, drug and alcohol addiction, and despair that led her to attempt suicide. But when she was fifty-three years old, Gert called out to God for help. She experienced the transforming grace of God through Jesus Christ. From that point onward, she couldn't keep quiet about the Lord, and soon she was traveling all around the country sharing her story of salvation.

When Gert finished her powerful presentation, the church erupted with applause. This was in the late 1960s, mind you, when Presbyterians didn't clap in church. But we had been profoundly moved by Gert's story and wanted to share our gratitude. Yet, as soon as we began clapping, she pointed upward and shouted, "Don't clap for me. Clap for God!" Our applause became louder as we stood, banging our hands together for the God who had saved Gert Behanna from destruction, and who saves us as well. In that moment I experienced for the first time the exquisite joy of unbridled praise. Though my lips were silent, my hands did all the praising. Along with a roomful of unusually liberated Presbyterians, I gave God a standing ovation. And I meant it with all my heart.

The lasting import of that moment didn't come from my feelings of ecstasy, however, but from my renewed commitment to God. I gave myself to him as never before. What happened that night wasn't just a fleeting pleasure. It stayed with me in the weeks that followed as I sought to live more consistently for God's glory. By praising God with my body, I was primed to offer him my body each day. I wanted to fulfill the biblical vision of embodied worship: "Present your bodies as a living sacrifice, holy and acceptable to God, which is your spiritual worship" (Romans 12:1). We worship God with our bodies, not just in our daily devotions or corporate worship services, but every minute as we serve him in the world.

When we clap and shout and do all the other things we read about in the Psalms, we offer up our lives to God. In this way we begin to live out the full commitment celebrated in this classic hymn:

Take my life, and let it be
Consecrated, Lord, to Thee.
Take my moments and my days;
Let them flow in ceaseless praise,
Let them flow in ceaseless praise.

Take my hands, and let them move
At the impulse of Thy love.
Take my feet, and let them be
Swift and beautiful for Thee,
Swift and beautiful for Thee.

Take my voice, and let me sing,
Always, only, for my King.
Take my lips, and let them be
Filled with messages from Thee,
Filled with messages from Thee.

Take my silver and my gold,
Not a mite would I withhold;
Take my intellect, and use
Every power as Thou shalt choose,
Every power as Thou shalt choose.

Take my will, and make it Thine;
It shall be no longer mine.
Take my heart, it is Thine own;
It shall be Thy royal throne,
It shall be Thy royal throne.

Take my love; my Lord, I pour
At Thy feet its treasure store.
Take myself, and I will be
Ever, only, all for Thee,
Ever, only, all for Thee.[5]

An Exercise in Prayer of Physical Expression

If possible, attend a worship service where diverse physical expression is encouraged. This may be in your own church, or you may need to attend a sister church nearby. Find a place where you can join with other believers in offering unabashed worship to God with heart, soul, mind, and strength. As you worship, ask the Lord for new freedom and joy. Don't think too much about yourself. Instead, think about God, about his greatness and mercy. Give him all that you are, even your body.

In your personal devotions, try using physical expressions that are unfamiliar to you. Kneel before the Lord in prayer. Or lift your hands to him. Once more, don't get too caught up in what you're doing; just let your body be an instrument of prayer.

I cry aloud to God,
    aloud to God, that he may hear me.
In the day of my trouble I seek the Lord;
    in the night my hand is stretched out without wearying;
    my soul refuses to be comforted.
I think of God, and I moan;
    I meditate, and my spirit faints. *Selah*

You keep my eyelids from closing;
    I am so troubled that I cannot speak.
I consider the days of old,
    and remember the years of long ago.
I commune with my heart in the night;
    I meditate and search my spirit:
"Will the Lord spurn forever,
    and never again be favorable?
Has his steadfast love ceased forever?
    Are his promises at an end for all time?
Has God forgotten to be gracious?
    Has he in anger shut up his compassion?" *Selah*
And I say, "It is my grief
    that the right hand of the Most High has changed."

I will call to mind the deeds of the LORD;
    I will remember your wonders of old.
I will meditate on all your work,
    and muse on your mighty deeds.
Your way, O God, is holy.
    What god is so great as our God?
You are the God who works wonders;
    you have displayed your might among the peoples.
With your strong arm you redeemed your people,
    the descendants of Jacob and Joseph. *Selah*

    —PSALM 77:1-15

GROANING IN THE NIGHT

Prayer of Desperation and Doubt

Though the house is still, my heart roars. It's after two in the morning, and I have to get up in less than four hours. But I can't get back to sleep. The worry that jolted me awake more than an hour ago won't leave. It churns and burns within me, holding my attention hostage.

I try once again to give my anxiety to God: *Lord, I can't solve this problem. Only you have the wisdom and power to do it. So I give this whole thing to you. Please grant me your peace and help me sleep.* But this prayer seems to go nowhere. It leaves my whispering lips only to drop onto my heart with a dull thud. God may hear this desperate prayer, but it doesn't seem like it.

Where is the God who comforts me? Where is the God who promises peace to those who trust in him? In my sleeplessness, it feels as if the Lord has gone deaf—or perhaps he has fallen asleep. Yet my desperate attempts to wake him seem to fail. In the distorting weariness of my soul, I wonder if God has forgotten me altogether. Or maybe all of this prayer stuff is just some cruel hoax. Maybe God doesn't care—if there *is* a God to begin with.

As desperation oozes into doubt, my prayers become less verbal and more visceral. When words fail, all I have left are sighs and groans. If I had the strength to turn to the Psalms, I could echo the opening lament of Psalm 77:

I cry aloud to God,
aloud to God, that he may hear me.

In the day of my trouble I seek the Lord;
> in the night my hand is stretched out without wearying;
> my soul refuses to be comforted.

I think of God, and I moan;
> I meditate, and my spirit faints. (verses 1-3)

How can we pray when we've run out of words? What does God want from us when we have neither the wisdom nor the confidence to verbalize a prayer? And what should we do when doubt invades our hearts like a deadly virus, seeking to kill our vulnerable faith? How should we pray when we're not sure God is there anymore?

What if doubt and desperation get the upper hand? What if faith is a ruse, God is a myth, and prayer is a waste of time—not even useful as a temporary stop to help us regain our shattered confidence?

These are some of the toughest questions we'll ever ask because they cut to the heart of faith. Fortunately for us, God answers our hardest questions in the Psalms. As we might expect, his answers aren't pat or pretentious. They aren't theology that is posited in a lecture, but theology that is proven in life. The psalmists don't tell us how we should pray in the depths of anxiety. Instead, they pray from the bottom of their own pit, recording their prayers so that we might join them in their desperation and doubt.

MOANING, GROANING, AND ROARING

Psalm 77 is one of twelve biblical psalms associated with or written by Asaph. He was a musically talented and spiritually sensitive man whom King David appointed as a choir director in the tabernacle.[1] This psalm was written during a season in Asaph's life when he was deeply troubled, though the precise cause of his pain is never explained.

Asaph begins by describing his desperate prayer to God: "I cry aloud to God, aloud to God, that he may hear me" (verse 1). Though he has been praying consistently for a long time, it seems to Asaph as if God has turned a deaf ear. Neither answers nor comfort have been forthcoming. Even at night Asaph continues praying, stretching out his hand to God (see verse 2). Still, he receives no sign of divine mercy: "I think of God, and I moan; I meditate, and my spirit faints" (verse 3).

The word translated here as "moan" means, literally, to "groan," "growl," or "roar."[2] It appears in Psalm 46 to depict the rumble of the ocean caused by an undersea earthquake: "though the mountains shake in the heart of the sea; though its waters *roar* and foam" (verses 2-3). Moaning in prayer may accompany words, or it may be all we have left to offer the Lord when our words run out.[3] Elsewhere the Psalms can speak of groaning or sighing in prayer:

> I am utterly spent and crushed;
>> I groan because of the tumult of my heart.
> O Lord, all my longing is known to you;
>> my sighing is not hidden from you. (Psalm 38:8-9)

The psalmists typically used words to communicate with God, just as we do. But sometimes the aching in their hearts exceeded their powers of expression. So they cried out to God, no longer with intelligible speech, but with gut-wrenching moans and sighs. Their example encourages us to do the same.

GROANING IN CHURCH

Many years ago Keith Miller helped lead worship at Hollywood Presbyterian Church. He was a friend of our pastor, Lloyd Ogilvie, and an author whose bold writings had spawned spiritual renewal across the country. In the middle of the Sunday-morning service, Keith rose to offer the prayer of confession. This was a standard feature of worship, which usually began something like this: "Gracious God, you have revealed both your holiness and your mercy in Jesus Christ. So in him we come before you today to confess our sins." But Keith began differently. Rather than using words, he moaned, out loud, very loudly. It might be more accurate to say he screamed. His ear-splitting "Aaaaahhhhh!" echoed throughout the sanctuary. Now *this* was a prayer of confession! It communicated deep dependence on God. It wasn't a cursory "Here are my sins; please forgive me." It was a desperate, visceral "Help me!"

To be honest, I'm not sure that Keith Miller's prayer helped the congregation confess their sins. They were so shocked that they weren't able to enter into Keith's sorrowful angst. And though I don't know for sure, I'd imagine that Pastor Ogilvie received more than one letter of complaint from disgruntled parishioners. Worship leaders just didn't get up in front of the congregation and scream, at least they didn't at Hollywood Presbyterian Church. But Keith Miller's nonverbal prayer illustrated dramatically what the Psalms exemplify. Sometimes we pray, not with the words of proper religion or even the words of heartfelt intercession, but with roaring that sounds like the raging sea. The best prayer in desperate times may very well be a wordless roar.

THE PRESENCE OF THE SPIRIT IN OUR GROANING

The psalmists' experience of groaning in prayer was picked up by the apostle Paul. In Romans 8 he said that we "groan inwardly" as we wait to enjoy the fullness of salvation (see verses 22-23). Suffering, inevitable in this life, leads to groaning. And as we are groaning, the Holy Spirit joins us. When we don't even know how to pray, "the Spirit helps us in our weakness; for we do not know how to pray as we ought, but that very Spirit intercedes with sighs too deep for words" (verse 26). Though commentators dispute the precise nature of the "sighs too deep for words," it's clear that Spirit-led prayer can involve nonverbal communication as we groan and sigh before the Lord.

Notice the astounding good news in this passage. Although we may feel utterly alone and cut off from God, in fact the Holy Spirit is with us, helping us and even interceding for us. Though we may not feel the Spirit's presence in our moaning, Scripture promises that the Spirit is there. God seems deaf and distant, yet he is right there with us.

As a pastor I have the honor of praying with people in times of darkest despair. I have witnessed the Spirit break through the walls people have built to guard their hearts, giving them the freedom to moan in prayer. In one particular prayer meeting, after I taught on the healing power of God, I invited those gathered to be quiet in his presence. After several minutes a woman named Arlene got up and said she felt led to pray for Lois, another woman in the group. I knew Arlene's spiritual maturity, so I consented. She stood behind

Lois and prayed silently. For a couple minutes nothing happened. Then, all of a sudden, both women began weeping. It was so obviously unstaged that I felt certain the Holy Spirit was at work. Before long both women were crying loudly, not with words, but with sighs too deep for words. Eventually they both stopped and were quiet again.

After the prayer meeting, I asked them what happened. Arlene was still rather stunned. She said that as she prayed for Lois, sadness overpowered her heart, and she couldn't help but cry. Lois then explained that she had been widowed at an early age. Though she felt abandoned by her husband and by God, she had always felt the need to cover over those feelings. She had never really told the Lord how much her husband's death had devastated her. And though Lois continued to live as a faithful Christian, something deep inside her had shut down. But when Arlene laid hands upon her, Lois felt her heart open vulnerably to God. As she wept, she poured out to him the sadness and betrayal that she had hidden inside for so many years. Without saying a word, she said it all, finally and completely.

That night the Spirit healed a deep wound within Lois's heart. After that prayer meeting, she was a changed person—still the Lois we had always known, but lighter, freer, more joyful. Her life illustrated the miracle of Psalm 30:11, "You have turned my mourning into dancing; you have taken off my sackcloth and clothed me with joy."

When We Doubt God

Asaph had his own deep wounds. And in the midst of his despair, he began to remember God. But his initial recollection of God's nature turned sour in his spirit. The contrast between who God had revealed himself to be and Asaph's own experience was too stark and unsettling. In this dark time, the psalmist began to doubt the fundamental nature of God:

Will the Lord spurn forever,
    and never again be favorable?
Has his steadfast love ceased forever?
    Are his promises at an end for all time?

Has God forgotten to be gracious?

Has he in anger shut up his compassion? (Psalm 77:7-9)

Some commentators see these questions as merely rhetorical. Asaph, they reason, was not actually doubting God's love and grace. But nowhere in Psalm 77 did Asaph answer these questions negatively. This is not a lecture in which Asaph "proved" God's faithfulness by telling the story's happy ending. This is not an inspiring tale designed to motivate us all to just buck up.

Though the psalm ends with a recital of God's mighty deeds in the past, Asaph seemed uncertain about whether God would act mightily on his behalf in the future. At no point did the psalmist stop to celebrate God's goodness in the words we find elsewhere in the Psalms: "O give thanks to the LORD, for he is good; for his steadfast love endures forever" (Psalm 107:1). No, Asaph could only hope that this kind of confidence would remain for another day. For now, all he could utter was the cry of an anguished, uncertain heart. When he uttered this prayer, he was still very much in process. By the end of the psalm, Asaph remembered God's saving works in the past, but they hadn't fully penetrated his heart in the present. What a precise picture of our own lives during times of dark doubt and desperate need.

But with Asaph, matters get even worse. In his raw and honest prayers, he reached a truly scandalous point. In verses 7-9 of Psalm 77, Asaph questioned the very core of God's self-revelation. In Exodus 34 God had revealed himself in this way:

The LORD, the LORD,

a God merciful and gracious,

slow to anger,

and abounding in steadfast love and faithfulness,

keeping steadfast love for the thousandth generation,

forgiving iniquity and transgression and sin,

yet by no means clearing the guilty. (verses 6-7)

But Asaph questioned the abundance and duration of God's steadfast love. He wondered if God had forgotten to be gracious. In other words, he doubted the validity of God's self-revelation as a gracious, merciful God. Asaph did not question God's existence, as we might today, but only his goodness.

Can you find your place alongside Asaph? Do you connect with his desperation and find yourself wondering what has happened to God? Have you ever doubted God's goodness and been bold enough to admit it to him? Have you ever wondered whether there is a God? If so, did you tell that to God?

I know some Christians who seem to be immune from doubt. It's as if God has given them a miraculous inoculation against the virus that infects most of us at one time or another. Yet most believers struggle with doubt at times. In his discussion of Psalm 77, the classic Christian commentator Matthew Henry observed, "Here is the language of a sorrowful, deserted soul, walking in darkness; *a common case even among those that fear the Lord.*"[4]

I'm a well-worn doubter, so I know all too well the contours of this darkness. I know how tempting it is to stop praying. After all, what am I supposed to say to God when I question whether he exists or whether he cares for me? Am I supposed to pray, *Lord, I don't even know if you're there to hear this prayer. And if you are, I'm not sure you care enough to pay attention?* If we take Psalm 77 seriously, then the answer is "Yes, exactly. Pray your doubts! Yes, question God's existence or his goodness!"

Whatever you do, don't stop praying. Don't turn away from God. Tell him exactly what you think and feel. I realize this can seem unnatural and counterintuitive, but, once again, the bold truthfulness of the Psalms teaches us to approach the Lord with no holds barred. When doubt grips you, don't loosen your hold on God.

The Prayer of Unbelieving Belief

The fact that Asaph included verses 7-9 in his psalm indicates that he hadn't given up on God completely. Even doubting prayer radiates from some tiny ember of faith, some lingering hope that someone is there to listen. Sometimes that's all you need, because in time the Spirit of God will blow upon that ember, causing it to flame up with renewed vigor.

As one who has often wrestled with doubt, I've always loved the story in Mark 9 of the boy who couldn't speak.[5] An evil spirit had possessed him, dashing the boy to the ground and keeping him from talking. The disciples of Jesus, usually adept at healing the sick, weren't able to help this boy, so they referred him to the Master. Jesus asked the boy's father how long his son had been suffering, and he answered, "From childhood" (verse 21). Then, in desperation, the father added, "If you are able to do anything, have pity on us and help us" (verse 22). Jesus replied, "If you are able!—All things can be done for the one who believes" (verse 23). Spontaneously the father cried out, "I believe." But then, as if zapped by doubt, he added, "Help my unbelief!" (verse 24).

Now there's an honest prayer, one I can echo with gusto. When I lay my hands on someone who has cancer, I believe that God *can* heal, and yet I can feel uncertain—"I believe; help my unbelief!" When I'm praying with a wife who has for decades asked God to bring her husband to faith, I know God *can* do this, yet we've prayed so many times before—"I believe; help my unbelief!"

In the story from Mark 9, Jesus didn't say to the father, "Well, I'm sorry. I said anything was possible for the one who believes, but your faith just isn't adequate. Come back and see me when your doubt is gone." On the contrary, Jesus cast an evil spirit out of the boy and restored him to wholeness. The unbelieving belief of the father was enough. Thus, if the honesty of Asaph doesn't give you the freedom to share your doubts with God, take your cue from Mark 9 and tell God exactly where you struggle. God invites the prayer of unbelieving belief.

Doubt is a frequent companion on my spiritual journey. Though I don't appreciate the company, I've come to accept it as an inevitable result of my hyperactive mind. I don't fear doubt as much as I once did. For, having wrestled with doubt for more than three decades, I know that God will ultimately cast it out of my soul if I continue to seek after him.

But I didn't always have this confidence. When I was a freshman in college, doubt sank its fangs deep into my heart. Though I had thought my faith was secure behind its protective cage of apologetics, it couldn't withstand the spiritual assault of "godless Harvard." After two months at school, I felt my faith slipping away, and there was nothing I could do about it. No matter how hard I tried, I couldn't make myself believe. The arguments that once convinced me to continue following God had lost their persuasiveness. For weeks I called out to God, often with agonizing tears. But it was as if he had remained behind in California when I moved to the East Coast. God seemed distant and silent at best, nonexistent and make-believe at worst.

Late one Saturday night I couldn't sleep. Worry over my waning faith kept me awake. Though I felt as if I had prayed all I could, it seemed as though praying was the only thing worth doing at such an ungodly hour. But because my roommate was asleep, I couldn't pray there. So I wandered over to the dorm's common room and entered the still darkness. Finding an overstuffed leather chair, I slumped into it and called out once again to my absent God.

Though my prayers of doubt had once been of the "I believe; help my unbelief!" variety, now they were more simply and desperately "Help my unbelief!"

"God," I said, "I don't even know whether you're there to hear me. But if you are, all I can say is 'Help me.' I can't make myself believe in you. My former strategies don't work anymore. I know all the best arguments. I can demonstrate that it's reasonable to believe in you. But none of these things touches my heart. Unless you make yourself known to me, I'm lost. Help me."

For many minutes I offered this prayer, both with words and with tearful moaning.

Then something unexpected happened. I felt a calming presence surrounding and embracing me. My desperate doubt began to drain out of my soul, replaced by the deepest peace I'd ever known. My tears of sorrow became tears of joy. As I thanked God for answering my prayer and making himself known to me, I began to feel joy unlike anything I had experienced before. It was like the joy the apostle Peter once referred to as "indescribable and glorious" (1 Peter 1:8). Waves of elation washed over me as I poured out praise to God. In those astounding moments, I realized that my life would never be the same.

And it has not been the same. Though I have sometimes wrestled with doubt since that night in college, the fight has never been as prolonged or as agonizing. Moreover, as I look back upon my life, I realize that my calling to full-time ministry began that evening. For the first time in my life, I wanted to offer my entire life—every gift, every moment—to the One who had so graciously answered my groaning for mercy. I wanted to help others know the God who revealed himself preeminently in Jesus Christ, and who made himself known to me personally in my moment of crisis. I also wanted to walk alongside others who wrestle with doubt so that I might help them know the God whose steadfast love never ceases.

Praying with Those Who Groan

As you read Psalm 77, you may not relate personally to Asaph's desperation or doubt. But even if your experience is different from Asaph's, you can still allow this psalm to guide your prayers. It can help you pray in fellowship with others who are struggling with desperation and doubt. It can remind you that even if you're enjoying a season of confident faith, others are struggling just as Asaph did. These brothers and sisters need your empathetic prayer.

Unfortunately, sometimes those who are doubting get our hardhearted rebuke instead. We remember the biblical injunctions to have faith,[6] but we often forget the commands to "weep with those who weep" (Romans 12:15) and "bear one another's burdens" (Galatians 6:2). The vulnerability of Asaph in sharing his struggles with us will help us join with those who doubt, so that we might walk alongside them and pray *with* them not just *for* them from our distant perch of superior faith.

Given my own struggles with doubt, it seems only fitting that God brought Tony into my life. I was a senior in college, by then solid in my faith and a leader in the undergraduate Christian fellowship at Harvard. Tony joined the group early in his freshman year. But soon he began to wrestle with doubt, much as I had. Things he had once believed so easily no longer made sense to him. God seemed to have disappeared.

For several months I met regularly with Tony. We talked endlessly about his doubts. I did my best to answer his questions and explain why I believed that being a Christian was reasonable. Tony and I would always wrap up our sessions with prayer. I had encouraged him to pray honestly, and he had been pouring out his doubt, often with tears of despair. I must confess that it wasn't much fun to pray with Tony. Week after week his prayers were predictably desperate. Sometimes I felt discouraged about his lack of progress. It seemed that doubt had conquered his soul. Yet I knew that I needed to keep praying with him.

Tony never had a transformational moment like mine three years earlier. But gradually he began to recover his faith in Christ. *Recover* isn't really the right verb, because what emerged from Tony's struggle with doubt wasn't like the faith he'd had before, but a deeper, more mature, and more lasting faith.

If you're grappling with doubt, I'd urge you to find at least one brother or sister in Christ with whom you can talk and pray. It might be your pastor, another leader in your church, or a Christian friend. But it must be someone who can handle honesty and raw questioning, someone who will stay with you through the agonizing prayers of unbelieving belief.

It might be hard for you to admit you're doubting. Sometimes those who share their doubts with me talk as if they're committing some unforgivable sin. But remember the freedom Asaph modeled in Psalm 77. And recall the desperate father in Mark 9, whose request was filled with unbelieving belief— and Jesus honored that request. Go ahead and allow someone to share in your struggle.

If you're not struggling with doubt, you probably know others who are. You may think of friends who aren't Christians but who are feeling the pull of the gospel. They aren't sure they believe, and they're filled with questions. Or you may know Christians who are going through difficult times and are wondering why God is so far away. Be sure to pray for these people. You may even feel led to offer to pray with them.

The God of the Desperate and the Doubting

What kind of God would encourage us to pray like Asaph, offering prayers of desperation and doubt? What kind of God would include Psalm 77 in a textbook for prayer? What kind of God would answer a prayer such as "I believe; help my unbelief!"? Only a God who seeks genuine relationship with us, not artificial religiosity. Only a God who desires humble honesty, not pompous piety. Only the God revealed in Jesus Christ.

I'm reminded of another episode from the ministry of Jesus. Once, when confronting those who "trusted in themselves that they were righteous and regarded others with contempt" (Luke 18:9), Jesus told a story about two men who went to the temple to pray. The first, a self-righteous religious leader, thanked God that he was a man of exemplary behavior. The second man, a sinful tax collector, was so ashamed of himself that he wouldn't even look up to heaven in prayer, as was common in that day. All he could do was pummel himself in desperation and cry out, "God, be merciful to me, a sinner!" (verse 13). It was this man, Jesus said, whose prayers were answered. "For all who exalt themselves will be humbled," Jesus explained, "but all who humble themselves will be exalted" (verse 14).

God is not looking for people who think they can impress him with their spiritual superiority. He's looking for those who come before him in neediness and humility, who open their hearts truly, doubts and all. In fact, it's precisely when we are weak, when we don't know how to pray, that the Holy Spirit "intercedes with sighs too deep for words" (Romans 8:26). When all we can do is moan before the Lord, the Spirit joins our sighing.

In Psalm 77, Asaph wondered:

Will the Lord spurn forever,
>   and never again be favorable?
Has his steadfast love ceased forever?
>   Are his promises at an end for all time?
Has God forgotten to be gracious?
>   Has he in anger shut up his compassion? (verses 7-9).

How should we answer these questions? No. No. No. No. No. No. The God who has revealed himself in Jesus Christ

>   won't spurn forever;
>   will once again be favorable;
>   is One whose steadfast love never ceases;
>   keeps his promises forever;
>   never forgets to be gracious;
>   and never ceases to show compassion to his children.

Even Asaph knew this. In Psalm 77 he revealed the depth of his despair. Yet in Psalm 73 he declared how God reached out to him, even in his bitterness and ignorance:

When my soul was embittered,
    when I was pricked in heart,
I was stupid and ignorant;
    I was like a brute beast toward you.
Nevertheless I am continually with you;
    you hold my right hand.
You guide me with your counsel,
    and afterward you will receive me with honor.
Whom have I in heaven but you?
    And there is nothing on earth that I desire other than you.
My flesh and my heart may fail,
    but God is the strength of my heart and my portion forever.
        (verses 21-26)

Even when God seems far away, he is continually with you, holding your hand. Even when your very life seems to fail, God is your strength and the One who will meet your deepest need…forever.

An Exercise in Prayer of Desperation and Doubt

Read Psalm 77, slowly and prayerfully. Put yourself in Asaph's shoes and walk around in them. Let his searching, questioning heart touch yours. Then begin to pray in your own words—or without words, if you prefer. Are there unexpressed needs or doubts lurking within your heart? Have you held back in your prayers, fearful that God wouldn't be able to handle what you really think or feel? Follow Asaph's lead and tell God everything. Ask the questions you need to ask. Open the channel for full communication with your heavenly Father.

If you are in a tranquil place in your life, without either desperation or doubt, then let Psalm 77 guide you to pray for others. Remember those who are struggling with circumstances that might allow Satan to attack their faith. Intercede for them from a place of empathy. Ask the Holy Spirit to guide you as you pray.

Save me, O God,
　　for the waters have come up to my neck.
I sink in deep mire,
　　where there is no foothold;
I have come into deep waters,
　　and the flood sweeps over me.
I am weary with my crying;
　　my throat is parched.
My eyes grow dim
　　with waiting for my God.

More in number than the hairs of my head
　　are those who hate me without cause;
many are those who would destroy me,
　　my enemies who accuse me falsely....

Let their table be a trap for them,
　　a snare for their allies.
Let their eyes be darkened so that they cannot see,
　　and make their loins tremble continually.
Pour out your indignation upon them,
　　and let your burning anger overtake them.
May their camp be a desolation;
　　let no one live in their tents.
For they persecute those whom you have struck down,
　　and those whom you have wounded, they attack still more.
Add guilt to their guilt;
　　may they have no acquittal from you.
Let them be blotted out of the book of the living;
　　let them not be enrolled among the righteous.

　　　—PSALM 69:1-4,22-28

O God, break the teeth in their mouths;
　　tear out the fangs of the young lions, O LORD!
Let them vanish like water that runs away;
　　like grass let them be trodden down and wither.
Let them be like the snail that dissolves into slime;
　　like the untimely birth that never sees the sun.

　　　—PSALM 58:6-8

SPEAKING THE UNSPEAKABLE

Prayer of Vengeance

One afternoon I was working in the yard with my daughter, Kara, who was five years old. As I trimmed the azaleas, a gentleman who lived across the street wandered over to say hello. He was a friendly man who sported a full head of elegantly groomed white hair. After he greeted us, Kara looked up and, without the slightest hesitation, announced, "You're *so* old!"

Our neighbor was gracious in his response. Laughingly he said, "You're absolutely right. I *am* old." Of course I was mortified. I determined at that moment to teach Kara what she should *not* say if she wants to make it in this world. She needed to learn not to speak the unspeakable.

I confess there have been a few times in my pastoral career when I put my foot so far into my mouth that it's a wonder I was able to pull it out. Many years ago I asked a woman at church, "Oh, and when are you due?" With a resigned look on her face, she said dully, "I'm *not* pregnant." As you can imagine, I learned never to ask "Are you expecting?" unless a woman's stomach is watermelon-size and she's in active labor.

As we grow up, most of us learn the rules of polite discourse—often the hard way. We understand that certain things just shouldn't be said. As adults, if we're eating dinner at a friend's house and don't like the vegetables, we no longer say, "These lima beans are gross!" Even if we think such a thing, we keep it to ourselves.

Just as we have learned to censor our speech among people, we have learned to do the same in our communication with God. For various reasons we've decided it's best not to share many of our thoughts and feelings with the Lord. Usually we figure out the rules of "theologically correct" prayer on our own. But if we don't, well-intentioned Christians are happy to help us understand that prayer should never be too forthright. We learn to bar our holds when talking to God.

But then we stumble upon the Psalms.

The Scandalous Imprecations of the Psalms

The Psalms are full of prayers we'd *never* dare utter. As we've seen already, the psalmists felt exceptionally free to complain to God, even suggesting that the Almighty had better get out of bed and get going. But even more scandalous than the laments are passages that scholars call *imprecations*. An imprecation is a curse with which we call down God's wrath on someone. It's saying, in a word, "God, get that person!"

Imprecations thrive in the Psalms like weeds in an untended garden. You hit the first one as early as Psalm 3: "Arise, O LORD! Rescue me, my God! Slap all my enemies in the face! Shatter the teeth of the wicked!" (verse 7, NLT). As you continue reading through the Psalms, you keep running into cursings. They show up in at least thirty individual psalms.

The existence and frequency of the vengeful psalms are deeply troubling. As Dietrich Bonhoeffer observed in his book on the Psalms, "No section of the Psalter causes us greater difficulty today than the so-called imprecatory psalms. With shocking frequency their thoughts penetrate the entire Psalter."[1]

Sometimes the request for divine vengeance is relatively mild: "Rise up, O judge of the earth; give to the proud what they deserve!" (Psalm 94:2). But often the imprecations sizzle with white-hot anger. Consider, for example, the following passage from Psalm 69 in which David minced no words when telling the Lord exactly what should happen to his enemies:

> Let their table be a trap for them,
>   a snare for their allies.
> Let their eyes be darkened so that they cannot see,
>   and make their loins tremble continually.

Pour out your indignation upon them,

and let your burning anger overtake them....

Add guilt to their guilt;

may they have no acquittal from you.

Let them be blotted out of the book of the living;

let them not be enrolled among the righteous.

(verses 22-24,27-28)

And that's not the only place in the Psalms where vengeance morphs into poetry. Perhaps the most artful of all imprecations is found in Psalm 58:

[The wicked] have venom like the venom of a serpent....

O God, break the teeth in their mouths;

tear out the fangs of the young lion, O LORD!

Let them vanish like water that runs away;

like grass let them be trodden down and wither.

Let them be like the snail that dissolves into slime;

like the untimely birth that never sees the sun. (verses 4,6-8)

When was the last time you asked God to turn someone into snail slime? Even if you really wanted to pray something like this, you'd be sure not to do it. Neither would I. As far as we're concerned, Psalm 58 speaks the unspeakable.

What are we supposed to do with passages such as these? They contradict our sense of decency, not to mention piety. More troubling, they seem completely inconsistent with Jesus's call to love and forgive our enemies. How can I love someone while praying that he or she will dissolve into snail goo?

It would be tempting to perform what Eugene Peterson calls a "psalmectomy" on offending passages, in which we excise from our personal reading— and certainly from public worship—those psalms that offend our sensibilities.[2] But if we believe that the whole Bible is God's holy, inspired Word, then we can't just overlook the parts we don't like. In fact, we probably have the most to learn precisely from those passages we find most distressing.

I'm convinced that the vengeful psalms can lead us to pray in ways we desperately need to learn. The uncomfortable imprecations help us confront not only who we truly are but who God truly is as a just, merciful, and forgiving God. Amputating the vengeful psalms not only cripples God's Word, but it also deprives us of a deeper, truer relationship with God.

Let's look at six ways the psalms of vengeance help us pray more fully and authentically so that we might have a more intimate relationship with God.

1. We Learn to Be More Honest with God

Psalm 137 closes with these infamous lines:

> O daughter Babylon, you devastator!
> > Happy shall they be who pay you back
> > what you have done to us!
> Happy shall they be who take your little ones
> > and dash them against the rock! (verses 8-9)

"This is raw hate," Eugene Peterson observes bluntly.[3] It's a passage upon which many Christians understandably perform a "psalmectomy." I remember when Psalm 137 came up as the daily reading in a Friday-morning prayer meeting with my elders. As I read the final verses of this psalm in prayer, I felt awkward and embarrassed, as if I needed to apologize for this psalm and explain away its scandalous content. Although I had read this psalm before, I'd never read the upsetting verses aloud in a context of corporate prayer and worship. I was tempted to excise the offending verses from my reading.

But I didn't do it. Peterson is correct in saying that such "psalmectomies" are misguided. "They are wrongheaded," he explains, "because our hate needs to be prayed, not suppressed."[4] Most human beings feel hatred at some point. We might hate a family member who has abused us, or a teacher who belittled us, or a public enemy like Osama Bin Laden. I first felt genuine hatred when, as a junior-high student, I was robbed by three boys wielding knives and chains. They didn't hurt me physically because I readily gave them my money. But they humiliated me and stole not only my money but my sense of well-being in the world. Though I never saw those boys again, I hated them for what they had done to me.

Hatred, even when justifiable, is an ugly feeling. It's nothing we want to put on display, which explains why we're not inclined to admit our hatred in prayer. We'd rather pretend it isn't there, even in the presence of the God who knows everything about us. Who really wants to say, "Lord, here is something ugly in me"? I certainly don't. In fact, I never once admitted to God my hatred of those robbers. I was too embarrassed to confess such an unsightly emotion.

Yet, as I've said before, God seeks us as we are. He wants relationship with the real you, not with some airbrushed image. Thus, if you feel even a twinge of hatred or anger or vindictiveness, or whatever emotion you'd prefer to hide, God wants to hear about it. And you desperately need to talk with him about it. Otherwise the negative emotion will fester, ultimately keeping you from intimacy with God and full participation in the work of his kingdom. As Eugene Peterson wisely observes,

> We must pray who we actually are, not who we think we should be. In prayer, all is not sweetness and light. The way of prayer is not to cover our unlovely emotions so that they will appear respectable, but expose them so that they can be enlisted in the work of the kingdom.[5]

When we pray who we actually are, vengefulness and all, we stop pretending before God and experience greater transparency before him.

2. We Pray in Solidarity with Victims of Injustice

By God's grace, most of us have not been victims of the violence that was familiar to David and the other psalmists. We live with a degree of freedom and safety virtually unknown throughout most of human history. Though I've been robbed a couple of times, I haven't been beaten, slandered, or tortured because of my faith or my political views. Thus, when I read psalms written by people who truly suffered, I find it hard to enter into their experience of harsh injustice.

I was first confronted by my limited experience of injustice many years ago as I led a Bible study at a community college in Los Angeles. The students who gathered to study were diverse ethnically, socially, economically, politically, and theologically. Apart from living in Southern California and believing in Jesus, we had very little in common.

One afternoon I was leading a study of Jesus's command, "Love your enemies" (Matthew 5:44). When I suggested rather glibly that God always helps us love those who hurt us, a man named Ricardo interjected, "Yes, but sometimes it's very hard to love your enemies." I agreed but once again made such love sound rather simple. Ricardo kept emphasizing how difficult it was. Finally I asked, "Ricardo, do you have a hard time loving your enemies?"

"Yes," he explained, "a very hard time." He then told a gripping story. When he was a teenage Christian in Central America, he was part of a Christian evangelistic movement. He and his friends shared the good news of Jesus with their neighbors. They had no political agenda. But that's not how the government saw their activity. Fearing that Bible-believing followers of Jesus would become politically uncooperative, local officials ordered Ricardo and his friends to cease their evangelistic efforts. They refused to comply out of faithfulness to Christ. Not long afterward, while they were holding a prayer meeting, police stormed the meeting hall. They grabbed the leaders, took them outside, and shot them. Ricardo somehow escaped. He ran home, gathered his few possessions, and began the long trek that ultimately brought him to California.

When Ricardo finished his story, I was deeply moved—and also ashamed. I realized how cut off I was from the real suffering of God's people. I committed myself to a new level of fellowship with suffering Christians around the world.

I can't say I've honored this commitment consistently since that eye-opening day. But as I've been praying through the Psalms, I've been led regularly to put myself in the shoes of victims of injustice and to pray in solidarity with them. Old Testament scholar Walter Brueggemann rightly notes that through the vindictive psalms, "the believer may join in the prayers of those who take God seriously and whose destiny is so heavy that they need others to join in these prayers with them."[6]

Thus the imprecatory psalms help us pray both for and with suffering Christians. They remind us to lift up victims of poverty and injustice. And as we do, we also learn to pray against the enemies of God.

3. We Pray Against God's Enemies

As I've been using the Psalms in my daily devotions, I've found myself praying against God's enemies. Now this might sound like an unwise practice because it would be all too easy for me to regard my personal opponents as God's enemies and therefore to wrongly pray judgment upon them. If you don't agree with my politics, for example, I'll be praying you into snail slime. Worse yet, if you oppose *my* plans for *my* church, then clearly you're worthy of some biting imprecations.

But when I speak of praying against God's enemies, I'm referring not to human enemies, but to the powers that lie behind them. In the book of Ephesians, we learn that "our struggle is not against enemies of blood and flesh, but against the rulers, against the authorities, against the cosmic powers of this present darkness, against the spiritual forces of evil in the heavenly places" (6:12). Therefore we must put on our spiritual armor and "pray in the Spirit at all times in every prayer and supplication" (verse 18). Through prayer we fight against God's true enemies, the spiritual powers of "this present darkness."

These powers do their damage in different ways, but largely through the "isms" that plague our society. Racism, materialism, relativism, narcissism— these are not just social realities; they are spiritual forces that wage war against God's people and oppose his mission in the world. Thus, when I pray Psalm 58, I ask the Lord to defeat the spiritual powers that oppose him and to "let them be like the snail that dissolves into slime" (verse 8). I not only pray in solidarity with victims of injustice, I also pray that God's justice will prevail over the various evils that victimize his people. Without naming the political leaders of the Sudan, for example, I pray that the murderous ways of that nation be obliterated in the fire of divine judgment. I pray not only *for* the tens of thousands of Christians who are enslaved there because of their faith but also *against* the spiritual forces of evil that undergird such an oppressive society. Of course, I must also ask the Lord to defeat those powers, such as materialism or pride, that have a grip upon my own heart.

When we pray against God's enemies, we're reminded of the goodness of God and the wickedness in our world. In his discussion of the "cursings" in the Psalms, C. S. Lewis remarked that "the ferocious parts of the Psalms serve as a reminder that there is in the world such a thing as wickedness and that it (if not its perpetrators) is hateful to God."[7] Thus, when we oppose evil in our prayers, we reflect the nature of God. We are roused from the drowsy tolerance of our culture to live more justly under God's reign.

4. We Surrender Our Vengeful Desires

The open vindictiveness found in the Psalms unsettles those of us who have learned to keep such feelings bottled up inside. When we first read a verse like Psalm 58:6, "O God, break the teeth in their mouths; tear out the fangs of the young lions, O LORD," the violence of the language shocks us. Yet the violence doesn't go further than this. As Dietrich Bonhoeffer commented, "Nowhere does the one who prays these psalms want to take revenge into his own hands. He calls for the wrath of God alone."[8] Bonhoeffer may have put it a little too simplistically, because the psalmists might indeed have wanted to avenge the evil done to them. But whether they wanted to or not, they never professed their right to take vengeance into their own hands. Instead, they surrendered this right to the Lord.

When David asked God to blot his enemies "out of the book of the living" (Psalm 69:28), he gave up the right to do the blotting himself. When David turned over to God his anger and desire for revenge, he renounced them. The psalmists offered their rage to God. "But such rage is not only brought into Yahweh's presence," writes Walter Brueggemann. "It is *submitted* to Yahweh and *relinquished* to him."[9]

Of course, human nature is such that we often try to pick up our rage once again and act upon it. But if we continue to pray in the mode of the Psalms, over time we'll fully surrender our vindictiveness to the One who claims sole right to act upon it. "Vengeance is mine," said the Lord to Israel (Deuteronomy 32:35). When we offer our own desire for vengeance to God, we give it to the only One who can justly execute it.

Because the word *vengeance* is a strong one, you may be thinking, *I don't have vengeful feelings.* Think about this: Do you ever want to get back at someone? Perhaps when your boss treats you unfairly, you enjoy thinking of ways to make him pay. Or when your wife hurts your feelings, you give her the silent treatment. Have you ever returned pain for pain? Most of us would never do something that is openly mean. We're too clever for that. But we're pretty good at gossip, or at using the sharp edge of rejection to stab the hearts of those who wrong us.

Don't wait until you have sustained some traumatic injury to begin offering your vengeance to God. Lay before him even the small hurts and your seemingly excusable desires "to just get even." Give it all to God and let him deal with the situation. As you do, you will lay aside your right to seek revenge, even on a small scale. You'll be empowered to turn the other cheek rather than slapping the cheek of the one who hurt you.

Let me emphasize once again another benefit of praying regularly through the Psalms. This practice will afford you ample opportunity to take an inventory of your heart. As you pray the imprecatory psalms, ask the Lord to show you any vengeful feelings you need to let go of. The frequency of imprecatory prayer in the Psalms won't let you hide yourself from God for very long.

5. We Open Our Hearts More Fully to God's Transforming Power

When we pray vindictively, we open our hearts to the transforming power of God's Spirit. We lay ourselves bare before the Lord, giving him a new chance to "have at us." Conversely, when we censor our prayers, refusing to speak the unspeakable, we keep our hearts closed off to the Spirit.

Sometimes we fail to tell God what's in our hearts because of pride. We don't want the Lord to know how needy, selfish, and, indeed, vengeful we can be. We dutifully parrot Jesus's prayer "Father, forgive them" when our hearts want to scream, "Don't forgive them. Give them what's coming to them!" By hiding in the fortress of pretended piety, we post a big "No Trespassing" sign upon our hearts. We say to the Holy Spirit, "Off limits!" Thus, we receive neither healing nor comfort, nor the kindness of God that leads to repentance.

But if we risk telling God the truth, then we also invite the Spirit to touch our hearts and transform them. I know because I've experienced it.

Many years ago when I was ministering at Hollywood Presbyterian Church, a man I'll call Jim was one of my closest friends. Over the years we had shared our lives even as we shared in ministry together. But one day, for reasons I still don't understand, Jim turned against me. He never would tell me what I'd done or said that injured him. He offered only superficial explanations for his behavior while backing away from our shared ministry and fellowship. I felt deeply hurt and betrayed. I shared these feelings with the Lord but received only partial comfort. My anger toward Jim continued to smolder.

One day I happened to be reading one of the imprecatory psalms. As I read, it occurred to me that I felt about Jim much like the psalmist felt about those who had maligned him. I realized that I wanted my former friend to pay for the wrong he had done to me. This revelation deeply disturbed me because I considered myself a forgiving person. But I saw my true self in the mirror of the Psalms. I was harboring feelings of revenge and just couldn't banish them from my heart.

As I began to confess these feelings to God, I sensed that the Holy Spirit was leading me to pray in the mode of the psalm I had just read. It was as if God wanted me to pray not just "Lord, I have these wrathful feelings about Jim" but "Lord, pour out your wrath upon Jim." In some hidden place within me, that's what I really wanted to pray but had never felt free to speak. Yet I wrestled with God for a long time about what he wanted me to do. In the end God won the match. I was convinced that he had put this psalm before my eyes because he wanted me to speak the unspeakable to him.

So I imitated the psalmist. I didn't hold back any longer. I told the Lord exactly what I wanted him to do to Jim. I didn't ask for teeth-breaking, snail-sliming, or anything that creative. But I did ask God in my own words to make Jim feel the pain he had inflicted on me. My prayer was a jumble of imprecation and confession as I laid my confused, hurt, bitter heart before the Lord. After several minutes in prayer, I dissolved into a pool of tears, feeling rather like snail goo myself. I couldn't remember when I had felt more vulnerable, more exhausted, more ashamed, and more broken before God.

I don't know what God did with Jim in response to my prayer. Of course, that's not my business because, by praying vengefully, I had turned the whole matter over to God. But I do know what God did within me. As I truly offered my sinful, sorry, sad, angry heart to God, the Holy Spirit lanced an infected spiritual boil deep within me. Lots of ugly junk flowed out, but in its place God's healing love flowed in. I felt his comfort as I had not felt it in the months since Jim had betrayed me. And by a miracle of grace, I even began to feel genuine compassion for Jim and a new capacity to forgive him at a deeper level than I had done before.

God has given us the imprecatory psalms to help us pray those thoughts and feelings we would tend to keep buried inside, where they will contaminate our spirits. Pious pretending doesn't fool God, and it keeps us from experiencing his transforming presence. The more we open the hidden rooms of our hearts to the Lord, the more he will make his home in these rooms, filling them with his light and love.

I hope you don't need to lance a boil in your heart today. But if you do, take up one of the imprecatory psalms (perhaps Psalm 58 or 69). Let God's inspired Word help you articulate what you haven't been able to say on your own. Then use your own words. Lay everything before the Lord, with no holds barred. Let God have your heart, all of it, so that he might heal and transform it.

6. We Experience Once Again the Grace of the Cross

Earlier in this book we saw that Jesus prayed from two of the Psalms as he cried out to his Father from the cross. "My God, my God, why have you forsaken me" and "Father, into your hands I commend my spirit" are both lines from the Psalter.[10] But in his moment of anguish and unjust suffering, Jesus refused to echo the imprecations of the Psalms. Though he had every right to do so, he did not call out to God to smash those who tortured and crucified him. On the contrary, he prayed, "Father, forgive them; for they do not know what they are doing" (Luke 23:34).

As Christians, we seek to imitate Jesus, including his extraordinary forgiveness. Jesus himself taught us to pray, "And forgive us our debts, as we also have forgiven our debtors" (Matthew 6:12). Then, just in case we missed the importance of forgiveness, he added, "For if you forgive others their trespasses, your heavenly Father will also forgive you; but if you do not forgive others, neither will your Father forgive your trespasses" (verses 14-15). So, as Christians, how can we rightly pray the cursings in the Psalms, when their vengeful spirit seems antithetical to the forgiving spirit of Jesus?

I can't fully resolve this tension, nor do I think it can be fully resolved this side of heaven. But I do wish to offer some guidance as you pray the imprecatory psalms in the shadow of the cross of Christ.

First, we ask God to punish those who have wronged us not because we believe God must do it, but because we believe we must be honest with God. Ironically, the fact that God has revealed his unlimited mercy in the cross of Christ actually sets us free to pray honestly when we have vengeful feelings. No matter what we say, we know our requests will be received by the God who is "merciful and gracious, slow to anger and abounding in steadfast love and faithfulness" (Psalm 86:15). This God can be trusted! Returning to my story about Jim, if I had believed that God is actually vindictive and harsh, I would never have felt free to unload my secret requests for vengeance in prayer. But because I counted on God's mercy and love, I knew that he would handle my requests in the best possible way. Thus, I felt free to share my heart without worrying about the consequences.

Because we pray the Psalms in light of the Cross, we recognize that prayer of vengeance isn't the end point of our dialogue with God, but only a means to more intimate and ultimately more Christlike prayer. Thus, honest imprecatory prayer leads to a deeper relationship with God and, ultimately, to a greater ability to forgive others. God alone can lead us from a desire for revenge to a willingness to forgive.

But what happens when we're stuck in the mire of hurt and hate, unable to forgive? Praying vengefully seems as if it would turn us away from the forgiving love of Christ. If we do it arrogantly and superficially, I suppose vengeful prayer might have this result. But when we offer our imprecations honestly and humbly, at least we are turning to God rather than staying distant from him. Moreover, we realize that we lack the capacity to forgive unless we rely completely on the One who prayed, "Father, forgive them." Dietrich Bonhoeffer summed up this point incisively:

Thus the imprecatory psalm leads to the cross of Jesus and to the love of God which forgives enemies. I cannot forgive the enemies of God out of my own resources. Only the crucified Christ can do that, and I through him. Thus the carrying out of vengeance becomes grace for all men in Jesus Christ.[11]

Ironically, offering our wishes for revenge to God actually brings us to the foot of the cross or, more precisely, to the pierced feet and hands of Jesus. As we ask God to punish those who have sinned against us, we realize that Christ took this punishment upon himself. Both our enemies and we ourselves find salvation only in Jesus Christ. He bore on the cross even the sin of our vindictiveness and unforgiveness. Thus, prayer of vengeance brings us once again to the cross so that we might experience afresh the grace of God in Christ. We realize how completely we depend upon this grace, and we celebrate how freely this grace has been given to us.

Therefore, prayer of vengeance leads not only to genuine forgiveness but ultimately to praise. In Psalm 69, for example, David asked God to do all measure of terrible things to his enemies. But then, after his imprecations, he remembered that God heard his desperate prayers: "For the LORD hears the needy, and does not despise his own that are in bonds" (verse 33). Therefore, David concluded, "Let heaven and earth praise him, the seas and everything that moves in them" (verse 34).

If your experience of grace seems stunted, if your praise lacks vigor, perhaps you have harbored unforgiveness in your heart. Let the Psalms—yes, even the imprecatory psalms—help you offer your heart to God more completely. Learn to speak the unspeakable to the One who already hears the hidden cries of your heart. Let his grace enfold, heal, and transform you.

An Experience in Prayer of Vengeance

Read Psalm 69 prayerfully, dwelling especially on the imprecatory section (verses 22-28). As you pray through this psalm, pay close attention to whatever the Holy Spirit wants to do within you. If you sense no need to offer personal prayers of vengeance, do what I suggested in points 2 and 3 above: Pray for victims of injustice and pray against God's enemies.

You may think you have no need to experiment with prayer of vengeance, and that might well be true. But don't jump to this conclusion too quickly. In my pastoral experience, I've known many people who have harbored vengeful feelings toward others, sometimes for years, without knowing what to do with those feelings. I'd encourage you to ask the Lord to show you if you have unexpressed desires for vengeance. If you do, let Psalm 69 give you the words to pray what's in your heart. As the Spirit leads, you may or may not feel the need to add your own words to the words of the psalm.

O give thanks to the LORD, for he is good;
 for his steadfast love endures forever.
Let the redeemed of the LORD say so,
 those he redeemed from trouble
and gathered in from the lands,
 from the east and from the west,
 from the north and from the south.

Some wandered in desert wastes,
 finding no way to an inhabited town;
hungry and thirsty,
 their soul fainted within them.
Then they cried to the LORD in their trouble,
 and he delivered them from their distress;
he led them by a straight way,
 until they reached an inhabited town.
Let them thank the LORD for his steadfast love,
 for his wonderful works to humankind.
For he satisfies the thirsty,
 and the hungry he fills with good things.

Some sat in darkness and in gloom,
 prisoners in misery and in irons,
for they had rebelled against the words of God,
 and spurned the counsel of the Most High.
Their hearts were bowed down with hard labor;
 they fell down, with no one to help.
Then they cried to the LORD in their trouble,
 and he saved them from their distress;
he brought them out of darkness and gloom,
 and broke their bonds asunder.
Let them thank the LORD for his steadfast love,
 for his wonderful works to humankind.
For he shatters the doors of bronze,
 and cuts in two the bars of iron.

  —PSALM 107:1-16

SAVORING LIFE

Prayer of Thanksgiving

When my daughter was in kindergarten, her teacher planned to have the students celebrate Thanksgiving by making—you guessed it— painted turkeys. But were they going to use brushes to apply paint to paper? No, that would have been far too neat. The teacher's plan called for the children to paint their hands with poster paint and then press their goopy, multicolored hands onto white paper plates. The teacher, realizing that this assignment could prove to be tricky, asked for parental assistance. I offered my body as a living sacrifice for the sake of my daughter's education.

My goal was to help the students create their turkey masterpieces without getting paint all over themselves. I quickly discovered, however, that kindergartners don't share my commitment to neatness. They rather enjoyed smearing paint not only on their paper plates but also on their clothing, and even on their parental assistant—me! It took all the leadership ability I could muster to keep the kids on task so they'd end up with brown, red, orange, yellow, and green turkeys—but not brown, red, orange, yellow, and green classmates. I was exhausted after just one hour of helping thirty youngsters complete their assignments and return to class relatively unscathed. And when it was over, I found that I had managed to avoid looking like the victim of a paintball massacre.

As I was escorting the last student back to her desk, she turned to me and said, "Thank you, Mr. Roberts." I was startled but somehow managed to mumble, "You're welcome." Only then did it dawn on me that she was the only one of thirty students to thank me for my herculean efforts. I couldn't help but remember the occasion in Jesus's ministry when he healed ten lepers but received thanks from only one. I wondered if Jesus felt a bit taken for granted, as I did.

I confess that too often I'm just like those ungrateful kindergartners. I can easily forget to say thank you to humans who assist me in life, and even to God who is the Source of every good gift in my life.[1] Why, I wonder, is gratitude the exception rather than the rule in my life?

BARRIERS TO GRATITUDE

You may not share my struggle with the challenge of gratitude. I envy the few people I know who revel in continual thanksgiving. But I don't know too many who fit that description. Most people are more or less like me: generously blessed but tight-fistedly thankful. What explains this odd inconsistency?

It would be easy to point to the absence of thankfulness in our society. Sure, movie stars gush with gratitude when they win Oscars and politicians praise their supporters, but overall we live in an increasingly thankless world. In spite of tireless efforts by parents of young children, "thank you" is a phrase that's notable for its rarity.

Blaming ingratitude on social mores only begins to scratch the surface, however. We must press on to ask why saying thanks is so rare. Busyness is part of the problem. When I'm hurrying from one task to the next, I easily forget to say thanks. Courtesy requires time, if only a moment, and time is a diminishing resource in our hectic existence.

But busyness doesn't fully account for our miserly gratitude. Many of us are not thankful because we believe we *deserve* the good in our lives. If, for example, someone gives me a shirt for my birthday, chances are I'll feel grateful and communicate my gratitude. But if I purchase a shirt, I won't feel especially grateful because I'm entitled to own the shirt I paid for. I might thank the salesclerk, but I won't feel particularly thankful. Thus, the more entitlement I feel, the less grateful I will be.

I witnessed a vivid example of this when I was a college freshman. I was able to attend Harvard because the school offered me a substantial scholarship based on financial need. A portion of this scholarship covered my book expenses and was given to me in cash. I simply needed to show up at the financial-aid office to receive my stipend.

When I arrived at the office, I joined a long line of students just like me. Since it took a few minutes to process each student, I realized I'd have to wait about forty minutes before receiving my money. But I didn't resent the wait because I was thankful for the assistance.

As I stood there counting my blessings, a student a few places in front of me started to get agitated. "They shouldn't make us stand in line like this," he complained. "It's such a waste of time." When he didn't get much support from others in line, he seemed to become even angrier. "Let's go," he moaned. "Let's get this show on the road. I've got stuff to do." Finally he lifted his voice to no one in particular and shouted, "C'mon. Just give me *my money!*"

Even I, so frequently ungrateful, was shocked. *My* money? Whereas most of us appreciated the fact that Harvard was willing to share some of *its* money with us, this student felt entitled to every cent. There wasn't an ounce of gratitude in his sad and spoiled soul.

Most of us aren't nearly as blunt in expressing our ingratitude; we're better at covering up our true feelings. But we often take God's blessings for granted, and when things don't go according to our plans, we easily get frustrated with God. Recently the air conditioner in my car stopped working, and I found myself unforgivably cranky. Consider the facts: I had a new car with air conditioning that would be fixed under the warranty on the following day. But I was angry with the world—and with its Maker. Gratitude disappeared in the smoke of my wrath.

I know I'm not alone. I pastor a church of people who are richly blessed by God. Yet when life's inevitable disappointments come along—a child doesn't get into the best college or someone gets laid off—some of my parishioners sink in the quicksand of self-pity. "Why is God doing this to me?" they complain. "Haven't I been a good Christian?" Translated, this means, "I deserve to get good things from God. They're rewards I've earned." Or, to borrow the blunt words of a former Harvard student, "C'mon, God, just give me *my rewards!*"

Thankfully, God has not abandoned us to our ingratitude. In myriad ways he rescues us from the error of entitlement and the sham of self-pity. We are rescued, in part, by the ancient Hebrew prayers in the Psalms. As David and other psalmists exemplify genuine gratitude, they urge us to join them. Thirteen times the Psalms call us to "give thanks to the LORD." One of these summonses to gratitude occurs in the first verse of Psalm 107, which shows us the nature of thanksgiving and also why we should give thanks.

AN INVITATION TO THANKSGIVING

"O give thanks to the LORD, for he is good." So begins Psalm 107. The rest of the psalm obeys this imperative. The Hebrew verb translated "to give thanks" has a root meaning "to throw" or "to cast."[2] In a sense, we toss our thanksgivings up so God might catch them. We are so grateful that we can't keep our words of thanks bottled up inside.

Appropriately, the first reason for giving thanks points to God's nature: "for he is good" (verse 1). The rest of the verse explains, "for his steadfast love endures forever." How do we know God's goodness and love? Through the inspired record of God's good and loving actions. Gratitude is a fitting response to what God has done for us, a response in which we acknowledge both the deed and the Doer. It's something we not only hold in our hearts but express with our lips. "Let the redeemed of the LORD *say so*," verse 2 urges.

The rest of Psalm 107 elaborates on the ways in which God has been good to his people and how they should thank him in return. It depicts four situations in which the Israelites, desperately helpless, cried out to God (see verses 6,13,19,28). Yet whether they were famished in the wilderness, locked in prison, sick unto death, or caught in a raging sea, God rescued them. He met their need even when their suffering was a result of their own sin (see verses 11,17). The Lord satisfied their hunger, shattered their bonds, healed their diseases, and stilled the raging storm (verses 9,16,20,29). No matter what the situation, however, the psalmist called for the same response of gratitude:

Let them thank the LORD for his steadfast love,
>   for his wonderful works to humankind. (verses 8,15,21,31)

The language of Psalm 107 interweaves the present experience of the chosen people with their historic redemption from Egypt and the personal experience of each individual Israelite. The immediate context for this psalm is God's gathering the Israelites after the exile in Babylon (see verses 2-3). Yet the four examples point backward from that divine work to the exodus from Egypt, when the Lord fed his people, delivered them, healed them, and brought them through the sea. Moreover, the language of the psalm is sufficiently provocative so that every person who has experienced God's grace could use it to express gratitude for personal deliverance.

As Christians, we see in Psalm 107 a conspicuous foreshadowing of Christ, who fed the hungry, set the prisoners free, healed the sick, and stilled the storm. Both the historic salvation of Christ and our personal experiences of grace find expression in this psalm. It enables us to join in a mighty chorus of gratitude, remembering God's redemption in the past and celebrating his ongoing salvation in the present. Psalm 107 teaches us to build upon our remembrance of God's mighty works by offering thanksgiving for past, present, and even future grace.

We are called not merely to feel grateful but to express our gratitude: "Let the redeemed of the LORD say so" (verse 2). Though thankfulness should permeate our hearts, this alone is not enough. God deserves to *hear* our thanks. And so do our sisters and brothers in God's family.

SHARING THANKS TOGETHER

Although Psalm 107 can enhance your private expressions of gratitude, its primary purpose is to encourage corporate thanksgiving. The "redeemed of the Lord" should say thank you, especially in the company of the faithful: "Let them extol him in the congregation of the people, and praise him in the assembly of the elders" (verse 32).

In private thanksgiving God receives the honor he deserves. In public thanksgiving that honor multiplies. When we thank God in public, others have the blessing of hearing about God's work in our lives and joining in our gratitude. Moreover, our testimony often reminds them of ways they have been blessed but perhaps have neglected to acknowledge to the Lord.

In a variety of congregational gatherings, my church facilitates shared thanksgiving. Sometimes, though, what gets mentioned isn't what I had anticipated. At one service that focused on God's holiness, an individual said, "Thank you for being a perfect God." Another added, "Thank you for setting us apart as your holy people." So far, so good. Then my six-year-old son chimed in. "Thank you, Jesus, that I could see the Godzilla movie today!" Not exactly what I would have preferred to come out of the mouth of a worshiper, especially my own son. I'm afraid Nathan rather missed the theme of holiness, forgivable for a six-year-old, I suppose. Of course, I was also afraid that others in the service would think I had let my young son watch the most recent Godzilla film (rated PG-13 for excessive violence) rather than the old black-and-white version (safely rated G).

There are risks in open corporate prayer, of course, but the benefits far outweigh the costs. During our annual Thanksgiving Eve service, we feature an open-mike time when any member can lift up thanks to God. I frequently find myself not only saying "Amen" to the thankful expressions of others but also thanking God in new ways myself. One time, one of the associate pastors, Larry, thanked God publicly for Johann Sebastian Bach. Like Larry, I am a lover of Bach's music, but until that moment I had never thought to thank the Lord for this composer and his music. On another occasion a young child said, "I thank God for my Sunday-school teachers." I began to remember my own teachers, who had helped me grow in faith and in biblical knowledge. For the first time in my life, I thanked God for Miss Kane and Mr. Morgan, for Mr. Istanbulian and Mr. Wherle, for Mr. George, Mr. Paddock, and Mr. Essick. As I silently spoke these names to God, I felt profoundly grateful for these dear saints who had made such a difference in my life.

Gutsy Gratitude

If things are going well in your life, you're probably eager to finish this chapter so you can start giving thanks to God. If you wish, put down this book and get started now. You can pick up reading where you left off. Helping you thank God is, after all, the main point of this chapter.

But you may be in a very different place today. Perhaps your life is heading for the Dumpster. Maybe you're suffering with a life-threatening disease. Maybe you've lost your job and wonder how you're going to support your family. Perhaps your marriage is falling apart or your adolescent son is struggling with drug addiction. *How,* you might wonder, *can I be expected to give thanks? Sometimes it seems as if God has forgotten me. How can I be thankful when I'm feeling so much pain?*

Life doesn't always prompt easy gratitude. Most of the time we struggle with an unruly mob of challenges and disappointments. Often we live with some degree of pain—physical, emotional, or both. And sometimes that pain can be almost unbearable. How can we be thankful then?

The Psalms don't answer this question with a logical apologetic so much as with a model of gutsy gratitude. In Psalm 86, for example, David prayed,

I give thanks to you, O Lord my God,
    with my whole heart,
and I will glorify your name forever. (verse 12)

In this instance, David was not expressing gratitude for an outpouring of blessing. Instead, he was giving thanks in the midst of what he called "the day of my trouble" (verse 7). His expression of gratitude came *before* his deliverance. Even after thanking God with his whole heart, David continued to lament, "O God, the insolent rise up against me; a band of ruffians seeks my life" (verse 14).

How could David be thankful when he was facing a band of violent ruffians? First, he remembered God's grace given in the past: "you have delivered my soul from the depths of Sheol" (verse 13). Moreover, he remembered who God is—past, present, and future. David was confident that the Lord who had revealed himself to be merciful and gracious would show mercy and grace in his own life. Thus David's thanksgiving didn't involve denial of pain. Facing his difficulties squarely, David nevertheless thanked God for what he had done in the past and for what he would do in the future—all of which recognized and honored God's unchanging nature.[3]

Many times I have witnessed gutsy gratitude like this. I think of a woman named Doris who, when she started coming to our church, was well into a battle with cancer. She knew the cancer was winning, but it wasn't defeating her spirit. Doris continually thanked God for his blessings in her life and especially for the gift of eternal life through Christ.

Doris's memorial service was filled with gratitude, but wasn't devoid of genuine expressions of sadness as well. A husband had lost his wife; children their mother; grandchildren their grandmother. Others of us grieved the loss of a dear friend. Yet in the midst of sadness, we experienced overwhelming, genuine thanksgiving for a life well lived, though it ended too soon. Most of all we celebrated the victory of Christ over death and Doris's glorious experience of that victory through faith.

The Psalms don't pretend that life is a bed of roses. In fact, as you read through the Psalms, you may wonder if the psalmists don't see life too often as a bed of thorns. You can't overlook the writers' stark realism about the sufferings and uncertainties of this life. But in the midst of their struggles, they turn their hearts to God, remembering his grace and hoping in his mercy. Thus, they express gutsy gratitude and influence us today by their example.

SAVORING LIFE THROUGH THANKSGIVING

Why should we thank God? Surely obedience to Scripture is one sufficient answer. The fact that God deserves our thanks provides another solid reason for gratitude. As John Calvin observed in *The Institutes of the Christian Religion,* because God "receives the honor which is due when he is acknowledged to be the author of good," and since we derive "all good from his hand," therefore "we ought continually to express our thankfulness."[4]

Yet, even though we offer thanks to God primarily for his honor, in the process we receive added blessings. One of these is increased enjoyment of life.

Taking life for granted is one of our most common bad habits. Usually we don't realize how much we do this until an unexpected event alters our perspective and surprises us with the gift of gratitude. I discovered this truth during my first Thanksgiving vacation as a college freshman. In September 1975 I left California to enter college in Massachusetts. For the next seventy-five days, I lived in a freshman dorm, a rather Spartan existence, but not an unpleasant one.

Since I couldn't afford to go home for Thanksgiving, I traveled by bus to central Connecticut to join some family friends for the holiday. On Thanksgiving Eve, as I retired to my room, I slipped off my shoes and socks to unpack my bags. I felt the carpet under my bare feet, enjoying the softness and the feel of the threads between my toes. Suddenly it dawned on me that I hadn't felt carpet like this since I'd left home. For two-and-a-half months, I had felt only dusty linoleum underneath my bare feet. But now, in a real home, I delighted in the sumptuousness of wall-to-wall carpet.

I had grown up in a home with carpet—bronze shag, to be exact. But I had never appreciated the feel of carpet beneath my feet until that moment. How could something so ordinary feel so enjoyable? I wondered what else I'd been taking for granted. That weekend in Connecticut added several other items to my list of newly discovered appreciation, including ceramic mugs, quiet nights, and a bathroom heater.

Thomas Merton, a prolific writer on Christian spirituality, sagely remarked, "Gratitude takes nothing for granted, is never unresponsive, is constantly awakening to new wonder and to praise the goodness of God."[5] Indeed, gratitude helps us slow down and savor life, much as we might linger over a fine meal to enjoy its pleasures. When we thank God for his gifts, we enjoy them doubly, both in the initial experience and in our gratitude.

As I have labored over this chapter, I've tried to expand my gratitude beyond its usual boundaries. In the process I've experienced greater delight in daily living. This morning, for example, I thanked God for the hearty taste of a cinnamon-raisin bagel, for the rich colors of wildflowers on a foggy morning, and for the sweet sound of my daughter's voice. By pausing to offer thanks for such gifts, I enjoyed life more today than I did yesterday.

If you want to experience life in all its fullness, take time to thank the Lord more often. Offer thanks for things big and small, for the usual as well as the unique. When you do, your experience of daily living will be enriched. And, more important, so will your relationship with the Author of life.

THANKSGIVING REAWAKENS OUR PASSION FOR GOD

Psalm 107 begins "O give thanks to the LORD, for he is good" (verse 1). Of course, God is good whether or not we give him thanks. How sad it is, however, that we who have experienced God's goodness can become so nonchalant about it. Usually new believers in Jesus exult in God's grace. But we who have been Christians for a while sometimes grow bored in our relationship with the living God.

Thanksgiving is one means by which the Holy Spirit reawakens our passion for God. When we remember what God has done for us and "say so," when we offer specific prayers of thanks to him, our hardened hearts can become tender once again. Yet even when we slack off in gratitude, God keeps blessing us in order to draw us back into intimate fellowship with him. As John Calvin noted, "God never ceases to load us with favor upon favor, so as to force us to gratitude, however slow and sluggish we may be."[6] Yet God's force is not heavy-handed coercion but open-handed generosity. God draws us back to his heart by gifts that spark genuine gratitude within us. As David prayed:

> I give thanks to you, O Lord my God, with my whole heart,
>   and I will glorify your name forever.
> For great is your steadfast love toward me;
>   you have delivered my soul from the depths of Sheol.
>   (Psalm 86:12-13)

Through constant demonstrations of steadfast love, God woos us so that we might thank him, not just with words, but with a whole, tender heart.

Some years ago a woman came to my church with a dulled sense of yearning. Though Sheila had once put her faith in Christ, ingratitude had turned her heart to stone. She felt entitled to every blessing because she considered herself to be a righteous person. Thus, she had no reason to thank the Lord, who, she believed, was only giving her what she deserved. But here's the catch: Sheila didn't understand why she had so little feeling for God. Her spiritual passion had long since burned out, leaving in its place only a dying ember of faith.

Before long Sheila's life began to unravel. Her health failed, along with her marriage. Her successful business hit the skids. At first she blamed God for her misfortunes, resisting the wooing of his Spirit. But over time God met her in her rebelliousness and brokenness. She began to see evidence of God's mercy and to realize that it was an utterly undeserved gift. For the first time in years,

Sheila felt thankful, and she told God about it. Thanksgiving opened her heart even further to the Spirit's transforming work.

After several months of grateful living, Sheila was a transformed person. You could tell just by looking at her. Her former demeanor, so dour and tense, had been replaced by a countenance of peace, even palpable joy. Sheila's renewal was a miracle of God, a miracle aided and abetted by her new practice of giving thanks. As she opened her heart to the Lord in gratitude, he softened and healed it. Not only did she find new delight in living, but she now delighted in God. And the more she experienced God, the more grateful she became.

I'm not suggesting that thanksgiving is some magic formula, that if you just say "thank you" enough times in prayer, God will be forced to revive your spirit. But I am saying that, in the mystery of God's will, our thankfulness opens our hearts to fresh experiences of grace. It's no coincidence that the New Testament urges us to pray "with thanksgiving," promising that "the peace of God, which surpasses all understanding, will guard your hearts and your minds in Christ Jesus" (Philippians 4:6-7).

CELEBRATING "THANKSGIVING"

If you were to ask most Christians when they celebrate Thanksgiving, they'd answer, "On the fourth Thursday of November." Little do they know that they actually celebrate "thanksgiving" more often and, I might add, more significantly.

Unlike the Israelites, we don't acknowledge God's grace by offering "thanksgiving sacrifices" (see Psalm 107:22). But we do remember the supreme, once-for-all sacrifice of Christ. In my church we refer to this sacrament either as the Lord's Supper or as Communion. In other congregations it's called the Eucharist. The word *Eucharist* is the English version of the Greek word *eucharistia,* which means—you may have guessed it—"thanksgiving." In celebrating Communion we offer thanks to God for salvation in Jesus Christ. We remember not the first exodus from Egypt into the Promised Land but the second and final exodus of humankind from death into eternal life. Thus, when we come to the Lord's Table, we are celebrating thanksgiving.

As we have seen, Psalm 107 pointed backward to the Exodus, the epitome of God's salvation in the Old Testament. It also foreshadowed the salvation yet to come in Jesus Christ. When we pray this psalm, therefore, we fill it with new meaning. We give thanks to the God who demonstrated his steadfast love in the cross of Christ. We are the ones redeemed by the blood of the Lamb, not from bondage to Egyptian tyranny, but from slavery to sin and death. The paradigm of our salvation is not the Exodus, but the cross of Christ. Here is the locus of our thanksgiving, our fullest Eucharist.

Nothing softens a hard heart, nothing restores spiritual passion, nothing fills us with genuine gratitude more than experiencing afresh the grace of the Cross. This has been true throughout the centuries. It was true in 1707 when English hymn-writer Isaac Watts penned the following words for a communion service he was about to lead:

When I survey the wondrous cross,
On which the Prince of glory died,
My richest gain I count but loss,
And pour contempt on all my pride.

Forbid it, Lord, that I should boast,
Save in the death of Christ, my God;
All the vain things that charm me most,
I sacrifice them to His blood.

See, from His head, His hands, His feet,
Sorrow and love flow mingled down;
Did e'er such love and sorrow meet,
Or thorns compose so rich a crown?

Were the whole realm of nature mine,
That were a present far too small;
Love so amazing, so divine,
Demands my soul, my life, my all.[7]

The power of the Cross to fill us with transforming gratitude also was evident in 1995 when English songwriter Matt Redman wrote:

Jesus Christ, I think upon Your sacrifice
You became nothing, poured out to death
Many times I've wondered at Your gift of life
And I'm in that place once again

And once again I look upon the cross where You died
I'm humbled by Your mercy and I'm broken inside
Once again I thank You
Once again I pour out my life

Now You are exalted to the highest place
King of the heavens, where one day I'll bow
But for now I marvel at Your saving grace
And I'm full of praise once again.

Thank You for the cross
Thank You for the cross
Thank You for the cross, my friend.[8]

Here's the ultimate Eucharist, the supreme thanksgiving, the source of inner transformation, the wellspring of spiritual passion: "O give thanks to the LORD, for he is good." Amen!

An Exercise in Prayer of Thanksgiving

Read Psalm 107 slowly, allowing the vivid images of the psalm to captivate your mind. If one of these images reminds you of something in your own experience, pursue that memory in prayer, thanking the Lord for how he rescued you. After completing your prayerful reading of Psalm 107, continue to thank God by focusing on the work of Christ, most of all his death on the cross. To this end you might wish to reflect upon the lyrics of the songs by Isaac Watts and Matt Redman.

Although this exercise may be done privately, your experience will be richer if you invite others—your family, your small group, or even your church—to share it. If possible, depending on the practices of your church, you might conclude this corporate exercise with a celebration of the Eucharist.

I will extol you, my God and King,
    and bless your name forever and ever.
Every day I will bless you,
    and praise your name forever and ever.
Great is the LORD, and greatly to be praised;
    his greatness is unsearchable.

One generation shall laud your works to another,
    and shall declare your mighty acts.
On the glorious splendor of your majesty,
    and on your wondrous works, I will meditate.
The might of your awesome deeds shall be proclaimed,
    and I will declare your greatness.
They shall celebrate the fame of your abundant goodness,
    and shall sing aloud of your righteousness.

The LORD is gracious and merciful,
    slow to anger and abounding in steadfast love.
The LORD is good to all,
    and his compassion is over all that he has made.

All your works shall give thanks to you, O LORD,
    and all your faithful shall bless you.
They shall speak of the glory of your kingdom,
    and tell of your power,
to make known to all people your mighty deeds,
    and the glorious splendor of your kingdom.
Your kingdom is an everlasting kingdom,
    and your dominion endures throughout all generations.

The LORD is faithful in all his words,
    and gracious in all his deeds.
The LORD upholds all who are falling,
    and raises up all who are bowed down....

My mouth will speak the praise of the LORD,
    and all flesh will bless his holy name forever and ever.

      —PSALM 145:1-14,21

FLOODING GOD

Prayer of Praise

A few years ago my wife and I attended a marriage retreat for couples from our church. The speaker, Christian psychologist Dr. Gary Brainerd, was well known for helping couples grow in their relationships, so Linda and I had been looking forward to the weekend.

During the retreat Gary got spouses involved in various exercises. One of these he called a "positive flooding exercise." The setup was simple. One member of each couple sat in a chair with plenty of space around it. In our case, Linda opted for the chair. My job was to stand in front of her, look her in the eyes, and say something positive. I could praise her appearance, character, actions, or whatever I chose. After offering one item of praise, I was supposed to walk around the chair and, upon returning to face Linda, make another positive statement. Then the process was to be repeated, numerous times. I was to "flood" my wife with praise.

I must confess that this exercise stretched me like an old rubber band that's been hiding for too long in the back of a desk drawer. It's not that I didn't have many wonderful thoughts about Linda. I did indeed. But I was not used to sharing them with her all at once. For some reason I'd always chosen to ladle out my praise slowly. Okay, you could even call it *stingily*. A compliment or two a day had always seemed ample.

Now I had to gush with praise even though that wasn't my typical way of doings things. But I do love my wife, and I'm usually a good sport, so I overcame my misgivings and began to flood Linda with praise. After a couple rounds, I started to forget about myself and focus more on her. This made the exercise much easier, and even rather pleasant. I liked telling my sweet wife lots of splendid things about her. She deserved to hear these things, and she seemed to enjoy it.

Just as I was beginning to get the hang of flooding, Gary Brainerd turned the tables on us. "Now those of you who have been receivers should become givers," he said. "Those who have been flooding need to sit and receive." You might think I would have liked this part of the exercise even better, but if you thought that, you'd be dead wrong. My inhibitions got the better of me, and I winced all the way through the second half of the exercise as Linda flooded me with praise.

I'll admit it. I've got issues when it comes to praise. Maybe the problem stems from my Northern European genes. My British and Swedish ancestors weren't exactly wired for being flooded with praise. Or maybe my discomfort with praise is related to the family I grew up in. When I was growing up, praise was given when it was deserved, but in neat, carefully measured quantities. My family members and I were always cautious not to spill when we gingerly spooned out our praise. We didn't withhold praise completely, but we didn't share it abundantly either, and *never* redundantly. That's just not how our family did things.

FLOODING GOD

My worship experience as a youth mirrored my family system. My church regularly praised God in worship services, but never for too long and never repetitively. None of those looping praise songs for us! A splendid anthem and a majestic hymn of praise—that was plenty of praise in one service, and it suited me just fine.

But being a praise-miser causes me problems when I get to the Psalms. In this book, praise is strewn generously all over the place. Moreover, certain psalms are, to be blunt, redundant with praise. Consider these excerpts from Psalm 145:

I will *extol* you, my God and King,
  and *bless* your name forever and ever.
Every day I will *bless* you,
  and *praise* your name forever and ever....
The might of your awesome deeds *shall be proclaimed,*
  and I will *declare* your greatness....
All your works shall *give thanks* to you, O LORD,
  and all your faithful shall *bless* you.
They shall *speak of the glory* of your kingdom,
  and tell of your power....
My mouth will *speak the praise* of the LORD,
  and all flesh will *bless* his holy name forever and ever.
      (verses 1-2,6,10-11,21)

You have to admit that this is repetitive. If I had written those lines, I'm sure my editor would have brought out the red pen to delete the repetition. It's just not good form to say more or less the same thing line after line.

How, then, are we to understand Psalm 145? Why did David go beyond simple praise to flooding the Lord with praise? And, more important, what does God want to teach us about praising him? What can we learn through the psalm's redundancy? How can this psalm deepen our communication with God and, therefore, our relationship with him?

A PRIMER IN REPETITIVE PRAISE

Psalm 145 is the only biblical psalm to be titled "Praise." The entire Hebrew title reads, literally, "Praise of David." Ironically, however, the Hebrew verb translated "to praise" occurs only once in the psalm, "[I will] praise your name forever and ever" (verse 2). But the whole chapter is filled with synonyms for *praise,* including "extol," "bless," "laud," "declare," "proclaim," "celebrate," "sing aloud," "give thanks," "speak," "tell," and "make known." Several of these verbs occur more than once.

Surprisingly, Psalm 145 doesn't include the common call to praise,

"Hallelujah!" which appears twenty-four times throughout the Psalms. This "Praise of David" isn't so much a direct call for others to bless the Lord as it is a testimony of personal praise: "I will extol.… I will bless.…" The purpose of Psalm 145, however, is similar to that of the more obvious calls to praise. The psalmist summons us to bless the Lord, not by direct imperatives, but by personal example combined with a compelling rationale for praising God.

The verb *praise* and its synonyms describe verbal expression of approval or commendation. When we praise God, we tell him how wonderful he is. Praise is closely related to thanksgiving, and the two frequently overlap in the Psalms.[1] But giving thanks tends to focus more on what God has done, whereas praise responds to who God is. This distinction shouldn't be pressed too hard, however, because thanks and praise are not tidy, but gloriously messy. Usually the psalmists praise God for who he is and thank him for what he has done, but sometimes they reverse the correlation.[2] Thanks can be a precursor to praise, as in Psalm 100:4: "Enter his gates with thanksgiving, and his courts with praise." But sometimes the two expressions meld together: "I will praise the name of God with a song; I will magnify him with thanksgiving" (Psalm 69:30).

No matter the exact verbs we use to express it, praise acknowledges the "glorious splendor of [God's] majesty" (Psalm 145:5). It proclaims his awesomeness, beauty, power, and grace.

How Should We Praise God?

Psalm 145 teaches us to praise the Lord with our words, not merely with our thoughts and feelings. David did "meditate" upon God's awesomeness, but only so that he might *proclaim* "the might of [God's] awesome deeds" and "declare [his] greatness" (verses 5-6). This proclamation happens daily, musically, and redundantly.

Praise Daily

"Every day I will bless you," says David (verse 2). The early Jewish rabbis tripled this expectation: "Whoever recites *A praise of David* three times daily will assuredly be a member of the world to come."[3] From a rabbinic perspective, not only are we to praise God thrice daily, but we're to do so by reciting Psalm 145.

I want to pause for a moment and ask you a basic question: Do you praise God each day? I wouldn't be surprised if your answer is no, because most Christians reserve praise for times of corporate worship. Their private devotions consist mainly of asking, perhaps with a touch of thanksgiving or confession sprinkled in. To be sure, praise ought to be a central component of congregational worship, but Psalm 145 suggests something further: the need for daily praise, even when we're by ourselves.

Praise Musically

In Psalm 145, as in our experience today, praising God involves singing. Those from many generations "shall sing aloud of your righteousness" (verse 7). The Hebrew verb translated "sing aloud" depicts joyous, robust, musical praise.[4] When we praise God with music, we unite our minds, hearts, and bodies in a joyful offering to God.

But what if I can't sing well? you might wonder. I've often been asked this question by people who claim they can't carry a tune. My response is simple: Just do it! Don't worry about how you sound, because God will be glorified in whatever joyful noise you make.

I always remember fondly the praise singing of my college friend Stanley. He used to belt it out with abandon, even though he could have been called "one-note-Stanley." From a musical point of view, Stanley's singing was atrocious. From God's point of view, it was a glorious, unpretentious gift of praise.

Praise Redundantly

I'll say it again: Psalm 145 is redundant. That might sound like a criticism, but in fact the very structure of the psalm is based upon over-the-top repetition. Psalm 145 is what scholars call an "acrostic psalm." Each verse begins with a different letter of the Hebrew alphabet, starting with the first *(aleph)* and ending with the last *(taw)*. The acrostic form of Psalm 145 usually gets lost in translation. You can get a taste of its unique flavor in the following paraphrase:

Ascendant praise I will offer to you, my God and King,
   and bless your name forever and ever.

Blessing I will give to you every day,
>   and praise your name forever and ever.
Colossal is the Lord, and worthy of colossal praise.
>   His greatness is unsearchable.
Declaring your mighty acts,
>   One generation shall laud your works to another.... [and so forth
>   through the Hebrew alphabet, until we get to the last letter of
>   the alphabet in the last verse]
Zestfully, my mouth will speak the praise of the LORD,
>   and all flesh will bless his holy name forever and ever.[5]

The form of Psalm 145 emphasizes completeness. "Praise God with everything you've got," it tells us, "from A to Z."

Not only would David happily acknowledge the redundancy of Psalm 145, he would approve as well of my description of praise as "flooding God." The first part of verse 7, translated "They shall celebrate the fame of your abundant goodness," reads more literally in Hebrew, "*They will pour forth* the memory of your abundant goodness." Praise is a gushing spring.

From David's vantage point, those who know God will naturally flood him with praise. This should happen every day without stopping. David promised to praise the Lord "forever and ever" (verse 2).

Psalm 145 teaches us to praise the Lord daily, musically, and redundantly. We flood the Lord with praise and never stop.

WHY SHOULD WE PRAISE THE LORD?

As I was working on the material for this chapter, I fortified myself with a snack from my favorite bagel shop. Looking around inside the store, I had to chuckle at their latest promotional campaign. Signs were celebrating my "inner bagel." "Support your inner bagel," one proclaimed. "Heal your inner bagel," read another. Then there was my favorite: "Glorify your inner bagel." This sign featured a drawing of a gleaming, crowned bagel surrounded by a royal court of coffee cups.

There is a problem with this campaign, however, apart from the fact that I have no idea what my inner bagel really is. Even if I could locate my inner bagel, would I really want to glorify it? Is my inner bagel worthy of glory? It may well need a little care, support, and healing. But glory? I don't think so.

We should glorify only that which is truly worthy of such an honor. We should praise only that which is truly praiseworthy. Inner bagels, I'm afraid, don't qualify. But God, on the contrary, is worthy of *every bit* of praise we can muster—and infinitely more.

Psalm 145 does more than model praise. It also gives us a rationale for offering praise. We bless the Lord because he has done "wondrous works," "awesome deeds," and "mighty deeds" (verses 5,6,12). These actions reveal God's nature, the ultimate basis of our praise. According to this psalm, God is glorious, majestic, good, righteous, gracious, merciful, loving, compassionate, reigning, powerful, everlasting, faithful, generous, just, kind, available, attentive, watchful, and judging. A God such as this deserves our praise, not just sprinkled, but poured out. He is the great King who deserves profuse declarations.

Praise knows no limits because there is no limit to the greatness of God. As David proclaimed, "Great is the LORD, and greatly to be praised; his greatness is unsearchable" (verse 3). The measure of our praise is God's own greatness. But his greatness exceeds our tools for measurement. We can't ever fathom the unsearchable grandeur of God. No matter how much we perceive it, there's always more that eludes us, infinitely more. Therefore, our praise never comes to an end, just a temporary time-out. When we think we're done praising, we glimpse even more of God's majesty, which calls us to praise him all the more. John Calvin was correct in his comment on verse 3:

> We only praise God aright when we are filled and overwhelmed
> with an ecstatic admiration of the immensity of his power. This admi-
> ration will form the fountain from which our just praises of him will
> proceed.[6]

And what flows from this fountain? Praise, flooding praise.

The Reason for Redundant Praise

Since we have only so many words to express our praise to God, we need to be redundant. Nonredundant praise is inadequate praise. *But,* we may wonder, *how can we find ways to bless the Lord that aren't so repetitive as to be tedious? Won't God get just a bit tired of hearing the same thing over and over?*

For me, praising God is rather like trying to find novel ways to say "I love you" to my wife on Valentine's Day. I've been giving Linda Valentine's Day tributes for more than twenty years now. During many of these years, I worried about being too redundant. I'd given Linda flowers, jewelry, clothing, cards, special dinners out, CDs of romantic music, and so on. *So,* I used to fret, *what else is there? What can I do this year that won't feel just like last year?* I knew to avoid useful appliances, Internet e-cards, or gifts I'd enjoy more than Linda would. But I still felt stuck, out of ideas and out of luck.

Then one year it dawned on me. Linda really didn't mind a fair amount of redundancy. I don't think she'd have appreciated receiving exactly the same gift or card year after year. But, all in all, she liked hearing "I love you" in just about the same words every year. And she was pleased to get a gift from me, even if it was just about the same as something I'd given her before. Linda was not so hung up as I was on the uniqueness of the words or gestures. Instead, she focused on my heart. If she sensed that I gave a gift out of love, that's what mattered. This realization set me free from the worry that had plagued me for so long. The words and deeds matter, I finally understood, but only because they communicate what's in my heart.

So it is with praising God. The Lord is more concerned with the integrity of our hearts than with the artfulness of our words. God isn't slighted by repetition. In fact he encourages it by giving us Psalm 145 to teach us to praise. Yes, we are also to sing a new song to the Lord.[7] But even our new songs are little more than reconfigured old songs. It's rare to find a new hymn or praise song that doesn't repeat what Christians have been offering to God for ages. I don't mean this as a criticism. It's a fact of life, given the limitations of language and the unlimited majesty of God. Besides, the new song we sing to God isn't so much a novel composition as it is an expression of a renewed heart.

BURSTING WITH PRAISE

When we encounter our gracious and majestic Lord, praise will flow spontaneously from our hearts and lips. Like it or not, we can't help flooding God when "we are filled and overwhelmed with an ecstatic admiration of the immensity of his power," to borrow Calvin's phrase. The more we see God, the more we praise him.

It's rather like what happens when you see a stunning sunset. As you stand there awestruck, don't you just have to tell somebody? You don't want to keep such beauty to yourself. You just have to praise the beauty of that scene to someone.

When my son, Nathan, was five years old, I took him on a late-afternoon bike ride. He sat snugly in a child's seat attached to the back of my bicycle. Before long the sun started to set, so I pedaled quickly to get home before dark. Out of the corner of my eye, I noticed that the sunset was stunning but didn't say anything to Nathan because I was busy trying to maintain a speedy pace. All of a sudden I heard Nathan's little voice behind me. "Dad," he cried, "look at the sky! It's *gore-jiss!*" Even a five-year-old couldn't keep quiet about that sunset!

How much more will we find ourselves bursting with praise when we glimpse the beauty, splendor, and sovereign majesty of God! We won't be able to keep it in.

If you're struggling to praise God, if you find the praise sections of your weekly worship service uninspiring, you don't need more caffeine. Nor do you need to rev up your emotions. Rather, you need to remember the One who deserves your praise. Reflect upon the nature of God. Recall his marvelous deeds. Consider most of all what God has done for you through Jesus Christ and how this reveals his character as "gracious and merciful, slow to anger and abounding in steadfast love" (Psalm 145:8). Don't focus upon yourself, but gaze upon the Lord.

Let me encourage you to attend to whatever helps you remember the greatness of God. It might be inspirational music. It might be quiet reflection. It might be worshiping with other believers. In my case, natural beauty helps get the living water flowing in my parched heart. When I'm standing on the beach, drinking in the vastness of the ocean, I can almost taste God's own immensity. Or when I'm marveling over the broad expanse of the sky on a clear summer night, I can join David's awestruck celebration of God's vastness:

> When I look at your heavens, the work of your fingers,
>> the moon and the stars that you have established;
> what are human beings that you are mindful of them,
>> mortals that you care for them?…
> O LORD, our Sovereign,
>> how majestic is your name in all the earth! (Psalm 8:3-4,9)

Praise flows generously from me when I'm in breathtaking natural settings. But even when I'm not, the potent combination of Word and Spirit lifts my eyes from the mundane and fills me with a sense of God's utter praiseworthiness. Praying through the Psalms guarantees that praise will rise to the top of your devotional life.

PERSONAL PRAISE AND BEYOND

Psalm 145 encourages personal praise. Whether we're in the midst of a joyful congregation or cloistered in our prayer closets, we should join with David in blessing the Lord.

Yet the more we recognize the greatness of God, the less we will be satisfied with praise that we alone can offer. God's majesty impels us to get others to join us. In Psalm 145, individual praise expands to include young and old alike, as "one generation" lauds God's works to another (verse 4). Moreover, David celebrated the fact that "all" of God's "faithful" and even "all" of his "works" will bless the Lord (verse 10).

Yet praise from the whole congregation of those who love the Lord still isn't enough. The faithful ones will "make known *to all people* [God's] mighty deeds, and the glorious splendor of [his] kingdom" (verse 12). In the end, not just the Israelites but "*all flesh* will bless his holy name forever and ever" (verse 21).

Why does praise of God keep spilling outward, from the individual to the believing community to all people everywhere? The answer points, once again, to God's nature and activity. He blesses his children, who bless him in return. But God's grace extends even further than this:

> The LORD is faithful in *all* his words,
>> and gracious in *all* his deeds.
> The LORD upholds *all* who are falling,
>> and raises up *all* who are bowed down.
> The eyes of *all* look to you,
>> and you give them their food in due season.
> You open your hand,
>> satisfying the desire of every living thing.
> The LORD is just in *all* his ways,
>> and kind in *all* his doings.
> The LORD is near to *all* who call on him,
>> to *all* who call on him in truth.
> He fulfills the desire of *all* who fear him;
>> he also hears their cry, and saves them.
> The LORD watches over *all* who love him,
>> but *all* the wicked he will destroy. (verses 13-20)

Notice the proliferation of "alls" in this passage. In Hebrew, the word *all* shows up seventeen times in Psalm 145, more times than in any other psalm except Psalm 119 (which has twenty-eight uses of *all* but is more than eight times longer than Psalm 145). Again and again in Psalm 145, David emphasized the lavishness of God's grace, which is showered upon *all* people. This explains why lavish praise, even from the whole congregation of Israel, still isn't enough. The "allness" of God deserves *all* praise from *all* people, and nothing less.[8]

AN EXPANDING VISION FOR EXPANDING WORSHIP

My reading of the Psalms in the past three years has expanded my vision for the praise and worship offered to God by my church. In the past I had been passionate about the worship of my own congregation, but not especially concerned to draw in our neighbors. Our church had other contexts for evangelism besides our regular worship services. I regarded "seeker-sensitive" worship dubiously, worried that some churches were downplaying God's glory for the sake of being inoffensive to nonbelievers. I was eager to make sure that our worship glorified God, first and foremost. What I failed to see was that God's glory should instill within us a passion to include all people in divine worship.

Consider these verses from Psalm 145:

All your works shall give thanks to you, O LORD,
     and all your faithful shall bless you.
They shall speak of the glory of your kingdom,
     and tell of your power,
to make known to all people your mighty deeds,
     and the glorious splendor of your kingdom. (verses 10-12)

The glory of God's kingdom moves his faithful to make his "mighty deeds" and "glorious splendor" known to "all people," so that they, too, might praise God. David in no way compromised God's glory in order to woo the Gentiles into worship. In fact, quite to the contrary, Psalm 145 accentuates God's unique sovereignty. The Lord alone is God and King, the One who cares for all, blesses all, and rules over all. The Gentiles are invited to worship God not on their terms, but on God's terms. They are called to praise not whatever god they wish in whatever manner they choose, but the one true God, who alone is to be praised.

God's grandeur cries out for grand praise from a grand chorus of *all* people. Therefore, we who know and praise God gladly accept the responsibility of declaring his glory among those outside the community of faith. Personal praise, when it is genuine, inevitably leads to an expanding vision for worship. The more you celebrate the majesty of God, the more you laud his splendor, the more you extol his unsearchable greatness, and the more you will yearn for all people on earth to join you. God's matchless glory deserves nothing less.

Thus, praise will impact every facet of your being. You'll praise God not only with your lips but with your whole life.

Praise: Your Purpose and Joy

According to Ephesians, God redeemed you so that you might "live for the praise of his glory" (1:12). A life dedicated to praising God, this is your ultimate purpose.

More than three centuries ago, Christians in Britain tried to answer the question, What is the chief end of man? Their answer has had a vast impact on Christian living ever since: "Man's chief end," they explained, "is to glorify God, and to enjoy Him for ever."[9] We exist not primarily for our delight, but for God's. As Rick Warren wisely notes in his book *The Purpose-Driven Life*, "Bringing enjoyment to God, living for his pleasure, is the first purpose of your life."[10] But by God's grace, when we live for his pleasure through praising him, we also take pleasure *in* him. That's ultimate pleasure, the best joy of all.

It's no coincidence that the psalmists rejoiced when they praised God. "My lips will shout for joy when I sing praises to you," proclaimed one psalmist (Psalm 71:23). Another added, "But I will rejoice forever; I will sing praises to the God of Jacob" (Psalm 75:9). C. S. Lewis, in his discussion of praise in the Psalms, observed, "I think we delight to praise what we enjoy because praise not merely expresses but completes the enjoyment; it is its appointed consummation."[11] Therefore, Lewis continued, the two actions of our chief end—glorifying God and enjoying him forever—turn out to be two sides of the same coin. Living on this side of heaven, we don't experience this convergence completely. But once we are in God's glorious presence, Lewis concluded, "we shall then know that these are the same thing. Fully to enjoy is to glorify. In commanding us to glorify Him, God is inviting us to enjoy Him."[12]

Even on this side of heaven, however, we begin to experience "an indescribable and glorious joy" through praising God (1 Peter 1:8). Praise lifts our eyes above the futility of this life. Praise turns our attention away from ourselves to the unsearchable greatness of God. Praise reminds us that God is "King of kings and Lord of lords, and he shall reign forever and ever."[13] Though we don't praise God primarily for our own benefit, praise nevertheless transforms our lives.

If you're feeling directionless, unsure of your life's purpose, start praising the Lord! If you're feeling dejected, weighed down by joyless living, start praising the Lord! God-focused praise is the antidote to so much of what ails us in our self-absorbed world. Praise sets us free to enjoy God now, even as it gives us a glimpse of the life yet to come.

A WINDOW INTO ETERNITY

Notice the conclusion to Psalm 145: "My mouth will speak the praise of the LORD, and all flesh will bless his holy name *forever and ever*" (verse 21). The day will come when God's name, once revealed uniquely to Israel, will be praised by all people without ceasing.

Psalm 145 points ahead to the glorious future of God, foreshadowing the vision of John in Revelation 5. In this vision, a vast multitude of heavenly beings sings praise to God:

> Worthy is the Lamb that was slaughtered
> to receive power and wealth and wisdom and might
> and honor and glory and blessing! (verse 12)

Then the congregation grows even larger:

> Then I heard every creature in heaven and on earth and under the
> earth and in the sea, and all that is in them, singing,
>
> "To the one seated on the throne and to the Lamb
> be blessing and honor and glory and might
> forever and ever!" (verse 13)

When we praise the Lord today, we rehearse for the mighty choir of the future when all creation will join together to sing praise to God. When we bless God, we get a foretaste of heaven now as well as the chance to get ready for it.

Notice that our praise includes the Lamb who was slain, Jesus, the Son of

God. When Christians pray Psalm 145, we can't help but think of Jesus, the ultimate revelation of God's grace and mercy, the One through whom God's glorious kingdom appears on earth. In fact, through Jesus Christ, full praise of the one true God has now become thoroughly Trinitarian. Thus, we join with Christians throughout the centuries by praising God in these timeless words:

> Glory be to the Father,
> and to the Son,
> and to the Holy Ghost.
> As it was in the beginning,
> is now, and ever shall be,
> world without end, Amen, Amen![14]

An Exercise in Prayer of Praise

Using Psalm 145 as your guide, meditate upon God's unsearchable greatness. Consider the breadth of his wonders, including creation and redemption. Allow the words of the psalm to highlight God's ultimate salvation in Jesus Christ. Then flood God with praise. Use the words of the psalm. Use your own words. Don't hold back. Don't worry about getting all your words just right. Be redundant. Don't pay attention to yourself; focus on God, on his majesty and splendor. And then "go with the flow." Let your heart pour out praise. Flood God with honor and glory, and enjoy him now, as you will forever.

Have mercy on me, O God,
    according to your steadfast love;
according to your abundant mercy
    blot out my transgressions.
Wash me thoroughly from my iniquity,
    and cleanse me from my sin.

For I know my transgressions,
    and my sin is ever before me.
Against you, you alone, have I sinned,
    and done what is evil in your sight,
so that you are justified in your sentence
    and blameless when you pass judgment.…

Purge me with hyssop, and I shall be clean;
    wash me, and I shall be whiter than snow.
Let me hear joy and gladness;
    let the bones that you have crushed rejoice.…

Create in me a clean heart, O God,
    and put a new and right spirit within me.
Do not cast me away from your presence,
    and do not take your holy spirit from me.
Restore to me the joy of your salvation,
    and sustain in me a willing spirit.

        —PSALM 51:1-4,7-8,10-12

Happy are those whose transgression is forgiven,
    whose sin is covered.
Happy are those to whom the LORD imputes no iniquity,
    and in whose spirit there is no deceit.

        —PSALM 32:1-2

THE DREADED ENCOUNTER

Prayer of Confession

I rushed from class to my car on a warm Friday afternoon in 1973. If I hurried, I'd get ahead of the horrendous freeway traffic that would begin to pile up at about 2:30. Hitting traffic would turn the routine one-hour drive to Mike's house into a grueling two-hour ordeal. Besides, I was excited about seeing Mike again. He had moved after junior high school, and we hadn't gotten together in a while.

Climbing into my 1964 Rambler, with a three-speed manual transmission and no radio, I made a beeline for the freeway. As I zipped along Verdugo Road, noticing that the price of a gallon of gas had gone up to a shocking thirty-two cents, something else caught my eye. In my rearview mirror, I saw bright blue lights glaring at me from the accusing eyes of a police motorcycle. I felt as if someone had dropped an anvil into my stomach.

I pulled to the side of the road to meet my doom. The traffic cop informed me that I'd been going fifty miles per hour in a thirty-five zone. My polite conversation and pleading countenance didn't soften the officer's heart as I had hoped. No warnings for this sixteen-year-old speedster. I got my first ticket. And the cop had the nerve to tell me to "Have a nice day." Nice day? Hah! He had ruined my day. (I didn't stop to think that I had anything to do with ruining my own day.)

I felt sick to my stomach all the way to Mike's house. It wasn't just the shame of having received a ticket or the thought of having to pay a twenty-five-dollar fine. What mortified me was the thought that I'd have to confess to my father what I had done. My dad had a perfect driving record. No tickets, no accidents, no warnings in twenty-five years of flawless driving. Now I, having been behind the wheel for only six months, had been caught speeding.

I wasn't afraid that my father would take away my driving privileges. He was usually quite fair, even merciful in situations like this. What I dreaded most was disappointing him. I knew that he was proud of what a fine driver I'd been, a chip off the ol' block. But now I'd ruined everything. I'd have to confess my failure to live up to his perfect driving record. I hated the thought of letting him down and dreaded having to face him with my shameful confession.

Have you ever done something that required you to confess your mistake to someone you dreaded disappointing? Maybe you messed up an account at work and knew you had to admit your error to your boss. Or maybe you wrecked the family car and looked ahead with trepidation to telling your spouse about the accident. Just about any human being older than two has approached confession with knocking knees and a sinking feeling in the pit of the stomach.

A Dreaded Encounter with God

That's how we often feel when we have to confess to God. We can remind ourselves that God already knows everything about us and that our confession won't be news to him. But our hearts still shy away from admitting our failures to him. After all, God is pure and holy—without even a quark of sin infecting his perfect nature. If I worried about disappointing my earthly father because he had a perfect driving record, just think about my apprehension over admitting my numerous imperfections to a wholly perfect God.

Even Christians who understand the wideness of God's mercy recoil at the thought of confessing their sin. We may be okay with admitting certain sins that seem fairly innocuous, but we tend to avoid confessing the sins that cause the most shame, the sins that have the greatest power to drag us down. Of course, by failing to admit them to the Lord, we allow these sins to retain their power over us.

It's natural to want to hide our mistakes. If I'm visiting your home and spill a bit of coffee on your new sofa, my first thought is that I could cover that stain with a throw pillow. Likewise, when I sin against the Lord, what I'd really like to do is cover up my offense, even though I know God has spiritual x-ray vision and can see through whatever fluff I employ to hide my sin.

David would have understood our dread of confession. In Psalm 32, for example, he admitted that he didn't at first acknowledge his sin to God, and then suffered due to his refusal to confess (verses 3-4). Although Psalm 51 is David's effusive prayer of confession, the superscription of the psalm informs us that this prayer came only after David had his dreaded encounter with the prophet Nathan. Like that motorcycle cop on Verdugo Road, Nathan confronted David with his sin and didn't let him off with a warning. David, who had gone to great lengths to avoid taking responsibility for a most grievous set of sins, came to God kicking and screaming. Confession was his last resort, not his first.[1]

We have in David someone who would be able to understand our hesitation to confess. I don't know about you, but I find this very encouraging. The prolific psalmist wasn't some spiritual giant who never struggled with the challenges that confront us; he was a fallible human being whose relationship with God was often just like ours. We aren't receiving a lecture from some master of confession. On the contrary, David resisted the Spirit of God just as we resist him. Yet he also discovered the blessing, even the ultimate joy, of confession. He shared his prayers of confession in the Psalms so that we might discover the blessings of confession.

We shouldn't be surprised to discover that when David finally got around to it, he didn't hold back. In Psalm 51, for example, he didn't speak in a way that minimized the offense of his sins. Notice his blunt, over-the-top confession:

> For I know my transgressions,
>   and my sin is ever before me.
> Against you, you alone, have I sinned,
>   and done what is evil in your sight,
> so that you are justified in your sentence
>   and blameless when you pass judgment. (verses 3-4)

David confessed not only to sinning but to having done *evil*. He admitted that God was completely right to find him guilty as charged. That's a no-holds-barred confession of sin!

You and I need this kind of boldness in confession. By carefully examining Psalms 32 and 51, we'll be instructed and encouraged by David's example. We'll learn not only how to confess but why confession is so essential to our spiritual health. We'll find not only new freedom in confession but a new desire to lay before God all of our sins, so that we might experience forgiveness, cleansing, and new life.

What Is Confession?

Before clarifying what confession is, I should first explain what it is *not*. Confession is not feeling sorry for having done something wrong, though sorrow usually accompanies genuine confession. Confession is not thinking that we've done something wrong and then keeping our thoughts to ourselves. Confession is not making excuses for our behavior at the same time we acknowledge what we've done.

As I write this chapter, a woman has just been found guilty of having murdered a man by hitting him with her car and failing to get help while he bled to death lodged in her windshield. The woman, though admitting the facts, blamed her actions on the combination of drugs and alcohol that filled her body on the night of the crime. In effect, she said, "I did it, but I'm not really guilty."

She's not alone in her pseudoconfession. We hear this sort of thing every day, from politicians and professors, from children and parents, from CEOs and CPAs. People blame their sins on their parents, their education, their ignorance, their deprivation, their victimization. You almost never hear anyone in the news come right out and say, "I did wrong, and I take full responsibility. Period."

Confession is, simply, telling God that you did wrong *and* taking full responsibility. Period. When we confess to God, we tell him in prayer where we have sinned by falling short of his standards. In Psalm 32 David said to the Lord,

Then I acknowledged my sin to you,

and I did not hide my iniquity;

I said, "I will confess my transgressions to the LORD,"

and you forgave the guilt of my sin. (verse 5)

The Hebrew verb translated "acknowledge" means "to make known." Of course, God already knew about David's sin, but David spoke as if he were informing God for the first time of what he had done. The Hebrew verb translated "confess" is, ironically, the same verb we examined in chapter 7 on thanksgiving. It comes from a root that means "to throw" or "to cast."[2] Context alone helps us understand the precise sense of this verb. When we're "throwing" our gratitude up to God, it means "thank." When we're "casting" our sin upon God's mercy, it means "confess." Both verbs used in Psalm 32:5, "acknowledge" and "confess," depict an open, verbal admission of what we have done wrong.

Notice the telltale parallelism in the first part of the verse: "Then I *acknowledged* my sin to you, and I *did not hide* my iniquity." The original verb translated "I did not hide" means, literally, "I did not cover." No pillow over the coffee stain here! Importantly, "I did not hide" employs the same verb that appears in verse 1: "Happy are those whose transgression is forgiven, whose sin *is covered*." We want our sin to be covered, but effective covering comes only from God. Paradoxically, if God is to cover our sin, we need to uncover it, to reveal it fully. In order to experience divine forgiveness, we have to do the opposite of what seems intuitively to be the right thing, hiding our sin.

Of course, we won't be able to uncover our sin to God unless we recognize it and first admit its wrongness to ourselves. We are wonderfully skilled at fooling ourselves into believing that we have not really sinned, or that if we have, it was an unavoidable result of some hostile power beyond our control.

When I finally told my dad about my speeding ticket, I had invented an elaborate story to minimize my misdemeanor. By the time I was face-to-face with my dad, I truly believed my far-fetched scenario. It went something like this: "Dad, I was driving on Verdugo Road, going the speed limit. But then I got to that part of the road that goes downhill for a mile or so. I ended up going too fast, not because I was trying to speed, but because I was going downhill."

Of course, my dad wasn't fooled by this pathetic excuse. He had often driven that same stretch of road without speeding. He knew very well that though my Rambler didn't have an automatic transmission or a radio, it did have brakes and a speedometer. I could have controlled my speed if I had chosen to do so.

In the midst of my embarrassing attempt to rationalize what I had done, my dad graciously cut me off. "Don't even bother with that story," he said firmly. "Just say that you made a mistake."

I considered what he had said for several moments, before finally choking out, "Okay, I made a mistake. But…"

"Forget about the 'but,'" my dad continued. "You made a mistake and that's that. You were wrong. You were driving too fast. Period."

My dad realized, wisely, that my excuses were neither honest nor helpful. If I was to experience his forgiveness, I needed to admit my error. Moreover, if I was to learn from what I had done, I needed to own up to my mistake. Finally, I did.

After my dad reaffirmed my confession of having been in the wrong, he added, "So you made a mistake. People make mistakes. That's just part of life. It's too bad, but it's not the end of the world. Now that you've admitted what you've done, you can learn from it and not do it again." And that was that. I never again drove too fast on Verdugo, even on the downhill parts! In fact, in thirty years of driving, I've become so adept at applying the brake that I've received only one other speeding ticket!

In Psalm 32 David said, "Happy are those to whom the LORD imputes no iniquity, and in whose spirit there is no deceit" (verse 2). Did you catch that? *"In whose spirit there is no deceit."* The way to genuine happiness follows the path of honest self-evaluation, not self-deception. Before confessing to my dad, I had to own up to the wrongness of what I had done. So it is in our relationship with God. If we're going to confess our sins and enjoy the benefits of confession, we must first see ourselves as we are—indeed, as God sees us. We must recognize our sin as sin so that we might tell God about it.

What Helps Us Confess?

Given the multitude of defenses we erect to keep us from honest confession, what will break through the barriers so that we might tell God the truth about our sin and experience his gracious forgiveness?

Suffering

The pain caused by our sin often leads us to confess. Suppose you say some nasty things about someone, and somehow the victim of your gossip hears about it. That person is hurt and angry, and before long you hear about it, either directly or through gossip. Now you feel the pain your sin has caused, both to your victim and yourself. This pain can lead you to confess, both to the person you offended and to God.

The suffering that follows sin is a form of divine discipline. Notice how David prayed in Psalm 32:

> While I kept silence, my body wasted away
> > through my groaning all day long.
> For day and night your hand was heavy upon me;
> > my strength was dried up as by the heat of summer.
> > *Selah*
> Then I acknowledged my sin to you. (verses 3-5)

David appears to have suffered some sort of physical illness after he sinned. Yet he attributed this illness not to a natural cause, but to God's heavy hand. The Lord was not punishing David vindictively but disciplining him so as to bring him to repentance.

You don't hear much about God's discipline these days. In popular Christianity God is viewed as a loving, forgiving Father, and indeed he is. But sometimes God's love is pictured more like politically correct niceness than genuine parental devotion. We tend to overlook the fact that loving parents discipline their children not to hurt them but to help them. So it is with God. As we read in Proverbs:

My child, do not despise the LORD's discipline
>   or be weary of his reproof,
for the LORD reproves the one he loves,
>   as a father the son in whom he delights. (3:11-12)

The negative consequences of our sin, whether naturally or spiritually induced, draw us to confession. God's kindness doesn't leave us stuck in our sin but leads us to repentance (see Romans 2:4). Of course, what we actually experience from the Lord may feel at first not like kindness, but pain.

The Holy Spirit

Many times, however, God graciously intervenes before we experience the suffering our sin deserves. The Holy Spirit convicts us of our sin, helping us admit, despise, and confess our active rebellion against the Lord.[3] In David's case, the Spirit spoke through a human agent, the prophet Nathan. This happens in our own lives as God uses preaching, teaching, and the exhortation of others to bring us to repentance.

The Spirit also leads us to confession by helping us see God more truly. In Psalm 51, David called out to God for mercy because he knew God was merciful:

Have mercy on me, O God,
>   according to your steadfast love;
according to your abundant mercy
>   blot out my transgressions. (verse 1)

God has not only mercy, but "abundant" mercy, enough even for a sinner like David, or me, or you. The Lord gives us not what we deserve but infinitely better than we deserve. Thus we confess boldly, not because we are bold people, but because we know that God's gracious nature inspires boldness.[4] This knowledge comes from the Spirit, who speaks to us through Scripture and in our own spirits.

Yet Psalm 51 also reminds us that God is a righteous and holy judge who cannot tolerate sin (see verses 4,11). We confess not only to receive mercy but

also because we can't have intimate relationship with God as long as unconfessed sin pollutes our hearts. Only confession will enable us to receive the full
benefits of God's grace. As John reminds us, "If we confess our sins, he who
is faithful and just will forgive us our sins and cleanse us from all unright-
eousness" (1 John 1:9). Specific confession of sins leads to forgiveness and
cleansing. Why? Because of who God is. Because God is "faithful and just."
As we walk with the *Holy* Spirit, we will be eager to set aside all that keeps us
away from our holy, righteous God.

Desire for God

The Spirit of God leads us to confess not only by helping us see God accu-
rately but also by reviving our desire for him. Consider these lines from
Psalm 51:

> Create in me a clean heart, O God,
>   and put a new and right spirit within me.
> Do not cast me away from your presence,
>   and do not take your holy spirit from me. (verses 10-11)

Can't you feel the yearning in David's heart? He recognized that his sin
had put a wall between himself and God. He hated the thought of that wall
becoming higher and more permanent. He longed for the wall to be torn
down so that he might once again experience intimacy with God.

Are you yearning for a deeper relationship with God? If so, then you will
want to cast away everything that keeps you from him, such as your sin. Confession of sin always accompanies a genuine hunger for God.

But what if you're not feeling much of a desire for God? Sin not only sep-
arates us from God but also desensitizes our hearts so we don't feel the pain of
this separation. There have been times when I have chosen to sin. In the
aftermath I can feel the dullness of my soul. I don't feel so much rebellious
against God as utterly apathetic about him. If there's distance between us, I
don't care all that much. In these spiritual doldrums, I call out to God for
mercy not only that he might forgive me but even more that he might restore
my longing for him.

So if you're feeling listless in your relationship with God, ask him to revive your spirit. Cry out not only to be forgiven but to be made new. You need not just a cardiac retread but a whole new heart. You need the miracle of the new creation.

The Miracle of the New Creation

David's prayer in Psalm 51 uses a curious verb. He said, "Create in me a clean heart, O God, and put a new and right spirit within me" (verse 10). The verb *create* is the same one we find in Genesis 1:1 when God "created the heavens and the earth." Throughout the Psalms this verb is used in reference to God's fashioning of the universe and its creatures.[5] Thus, in Psalm 51 David asked not only to be forgiven and cleansed but also to be newly created through God's divine power. As John Calvin observed in his commentary on this verse, "By employing the term *create,* [David] expresses his persuasion that nothing less than a miracle could effect his reformation, and emphatically declares that repentance is the gift of God."[6]

In seeking the miracle of new creation, David anticipated the coming work of Christ. About a thousand years after David penned Psalm 51, the apostle Paul wrote to the Corinthians:

> So if anyone is in Christ, *there is a new creation:* everything old has
> passed away; see, *everything has become new!* All this is from God, who
> reconciled us to himself through Christ.... For our sake [God] made
> [Christ] to be sin who knew no sin, so that in him we might become
> the righteousness of God. (2 Corinthians 5:17-18,21)

When we first put our trust in Jesus Christ, we begin to live in the new creation, tasting a bit of God's future as we are fully reconciled to God. When sin disrupts that reconciliation, confession nullifies sin's power, enabling us to experience even more of the new creation in Christ. Through the work of Christ and the power of the Spirit, God continues to do in us that for which David longed: He recreates us in the divine image, giving us a clean, new, sinless heart.

As we live in the new creation, experiencing through the Spirit the life of the future, reconciliation with God through Christ becomes more than a theological reality. It becomes a blessed part of our normal experience. Because we have been forgiven, we can enjoy God's presence even as he enjoys ours. We experience freedom not just from the stain of sin but from the desire to sin. This freedom isn't complete on this side of heaven, but it does give us increasing desire and power to turn our backs on sin as we turn our faces to the Lord.

In the new creation, God is our Refuge and Deliverer. In God we find safety and security. As Psalm 32:7 affirms to the Lord, "You are my hiding place; you will protect me from trouble and surround me with songs of deliverance" (NIV). This profession of God's protection comes *after* David confessed his sin and experienced God's forgiveness. The psalm makes explicit the connection between confession, forgiveness, and the blessing of divine protection:

> Then I acknowledged my sin to you…
>> and you forgave the guilt of my sin.
> *Therefore* let all who are faithful offer prayer to you…
> You are a hiding place for me. (verses 5-7)

Psalm 32 ends with a joyful affirmation of the protection of God's steadfast love:

> Many are the torments of the wicked,
>> but steadfast love surrounds those who trust in the LORD.
> Be glad in the LORD and rejoice, O righteous,
>> and shout for joy, all you upright in heart. (verses 10-11)

In the new creation, confession leads to forgiveness, which leads to reassurance of God's protection, which leads to joy, riotous joy.

JOYFUL BONES

The confession of Psalm 32 concludes with a call to rejoice in the God who forgives sins. Psalm 51 also shows that confession of sin leads to joy. David prayed:

Purge me with hyssop, and I shall be clean;
> wash me, and I shall be whiter than snow.
Let me hear joy and gladness;
> let the bones you have crushed rejoice. (verses 7-8)

This is not some superficial happiness, but joy that permeates our whole being, right down to the bones.

Would you like to rejoice in every part of your being? Then confess your sins to the Lord. The path to pervasive joy is not an easy one, but the destination makes the journey worthwhile. Consider Matthew Henry's comment on Psalm 32:

> It is very difficult to bring sinful man humbly to accept free mercy, with a full confession of his sins and self-condemnation. But the true and only way to peace of conscience, is, to confess our sins, that they may be forgiven; to declare them that we may be justified. Although repentance and confession do not merit the pardon of transgression, they are needful to the real enjoyment of forgiving mercy. And *what tongue can tell the happiness of that hour,* when the soul, oppressed by sin, is enabled freely to pour forth its sorrows before God, and to take hold of his covenanted mercy in Christ Jesus![7]

This echoes David's own exultation in Psalm 32:

> Happy are those whose transgression is forgiven,
> > whose sin is covered.
> Happy are those to whom the LORD imputes no iniquity,
> > and in whose spirit there is no deceit. (verses 1-2)

This happiness isn't the superficial glee of temporary pleasure, but the deep joy of eternal forgiveness.

The result of confession reminds me of what happens when I go backpacking. There's just about nothing in life that gives me greater delight than being in the Sierra Nevada mountains of California. I love to gaze upon the lofty, jagged peaks presiding over their court of deep green forests and cobalt blue lakes. My love for these mountains has motivated me to backpack among them, carrying all that I need for living in a high-tech pack attached to my back.

The hardest part of backpacking, as you might imagine, is carrying the pack. Mine usually weighs at least forty pounds, quite a bit more when I'm camping with my children and carrying extra items for them. After several hours lugging my pack up steep trails, my hips and shoulders feel as if I'm Atlas bearing the whole world on my back. Rather than enjoying the exquisite surroundings, I'm focused on the dusty trail in front of me. Each step forward is powered by one abiding thought: *Soon we'll get to our destination, and I'll be able to put down this pack.*

The feeling of shedding a backpack after a long hike is one of life's sublime pleasures. It seems as if the laws of gravity have miraculously changed and I could almost float. A lightness of heart follows the lightness of body as I begin to drink in the unsurpassed beauty of the High Sierra. Without the burden of my pack, I'm able to savor the richness of life. I feel astoundingly free, vigorously alive.

So it is when we confess our sins. When we finally unload the dead weight that has been dragging us down, we feel light in spirit, as if we might float up into heaven. But rather than escaping from this life, we relish it anew. Without the distorting, depressing burden of sin, we experience new joy in daily living. This joy sinks deep down, right into our bones.

Are you carrying a load of unconfessed sin? Are you tired of that burden? Do you want to be free to enjoy the Lord and therefore to enjoy the abundant life he gives? Then drop your burden at the foot of the cross. Confess your sins. Don't hold back. New creation is yours in Christ. "Be glad in the LORD and rejoice" (Psalm 32:11).

An Exercise in Prayer of Confession

If you're like most Christians, you haven't spent an extended time in confession for a while. Perhaps you've never done it in your life. Well, either way, it's past time.

Let me encourage you to set aside at least two hours for prayer in a place where you can be alone with God. Turn off your cell phone and remove all other potential distractions. Begin by reading Psalms 32 and 51 prayerfully. Let the prayers of David sink into your heart. If certain words or verses from the Psalms spark something within you, reflect upon what the Holy Spirit is saying to you.

Then ask the Spirit to guide your confession. Lay your sins before the Lord, specifically, honestly. Chances are that you'll begin with obvious sins. But when you seem to have run out of things to confess, continue to wait upon God. It's likely that the Spirit will bring other sins to mind. As this happens, offer them up in prayer.

You may very well come upon a sin you'd rather not mention. Even the thought of it fills you with shame. If so, ask God for the courage to be honest with him. Remember that you can't surprise him with secret sins but that he is eager to surprise you with his abundant mercy.

When it seems that you have finished confessing, return to Psalm 32. As you read this psalm, ask the Lord to give you his joy. Accept his forgiveness with glad thanksgiving.

O come, let us sing to the LORD;
 let us make a joyful noise to the rock of our salvation!
Let us come into his presence with thanksgiving;
 let us make a joyful noise to him with songs of praise!
For the LORD is a great God,
 and a great King above all gods.
In his hand are the depths of the earth;
 the heights of the mountains are his also.
The sea is his, for he made it,
 and the dry land, which his hands have formed.

O come, let us worship and bow down,
 let us kneel before the LORD, our Maker!
For he is our God,
 and we are the people of his pasture,
 and the sheep of his hand.

  —PSALM 95:1-7

O sing to the LORD a new song;
 sing to the LORD, all the earth.
Sing to the LORD, bless his name;
 tell of his salvation from day to day.
Declare his glory among the nations,
 his marvelous works among all the peoples.
For great is the LORD, and greatly to be praised;
 he is to be revered above all gods.
For all the gods of the peoples are idols,
 but the LORD made the heavens.
Honor and majesty are before him;
 strength and beauty are in his sanctuary.

Ascribe to the LORD, O families of the peoples,
 ascribe to the LORD glory and strength....
Worship the LORD in holy splendor;
 tremble before him, all the earth.

Say among the nations, "The LORD is king!
 The world is firmly established; it shall never be moved.
 He will judge the peoples with equity."

  —PSALM 96:1-7,9-10

FACEDOWN BEFORE THE KING

Prayer of Worship

In the classic Rodgers and Hammerstein musical *The King and I,* a young Englishwoman travels far from her homeland to become the tutor for the children of the king of Siam. Anna struggles to appreciate some of the Siamese customs, including the reverent submission shown by the people to King Mongkut. Whenever he draws near, his subjects fall to their knees, noses to the ground, in a gesture of humble devotion. The king's authority is absolute. His wish is everyone's command. In fact, he usually doesn't even need to clarify his orders. A simple command followed by "et cetera, et cetera" gets the job done.

Even though Anna grew up under the rule of the British monarch, she is shocked by the blind subservience of the Siamese people to their king. In her obstinacy, she refuses to render appropriate submission, and she challenges the king's judgment. Although she is willing to bow politely before King Mongkut, Anna refuses to fall to her knees, either in body or in heart.[1]

And we, the audience, cheer her on enthusiastically. Like Anna, we recoil at the sight of unreserved, reverent submission.

RETICENT ABOUT REVERENCE

Our discomfort with the idea of submission actually exceeds Anna's. She lived, after all, as a loyal subject of Britain's Queen Victoria, no minor sovereign. But we live in a democratic world, in an age dominated by egalitarian values. We are reticent to offer reverence or submission to anyone.

Reverence—a feeling of profound awe and respect—is as rare as a rotary-dial telephone these days. My friend Tim once appeared before the U.S. Supreme Court to argue a case. Though he didn't bow before the justices, he felt profound respect and communicated this through word and action. Faithful Catholics who meet the Pope kneel to kiss his ring. But that's about as far as reverent submission goes in the Western world. Oh, I did forget the scene from the sophomoric movie *Wayne's World,* where Wayne and Garth bow to the ground before their rock idol Alice Cooper, droning, "We're not worthy. We're not worthy."[2] The absurdity of this scene strengthens my point about the rareness of genuine reverence in our culture.

Ironically, the media are filled with images of reverent submission as our attention has turned toward Islam. We've all seen video footage of Muslims in prayer, kneeling on mats as they lower their faces to the ground in the direction of Mecca. This posture of submission to Allah perfectly illustrates the sense of the word *Islam,* which in Arabic means "submission." Literally, a Muslim is one who "submits" to Allah. If submission is rare in the Western world, it permeates the Middle East, North Africa, and Southeast Asia, where Islam predominates.

Given our experience of Islamic terrorism, however, Westerners are understandably guarded about Islam and all it represents. Devoted submission, even to God, seems to be a dangerous practice—far from the safe, predictable ideals of Western democracy.

But our democratic, egalitarian ethos affects far more than just our government and political system. The West's allergy to submission has influenced even the way Christians relate to God. Not long ago it was common for believers to kneel in prayer. Now it's the exception—at least in most Protestant churches. In the past, worship services were designed, above all, to foster reverence before God. Worshipers wore their "Sunday best" to church and kept silence during services. The booming organ inspired awe, as did the age-old words of classic hymns. Most churches encouraged bowing before God in humility, lowering heads if not bending knees. Even the architecture of church sanctuaries inspired awe-filled respect before almighty God.

Today, sanctuaries have been replaced by "celebration centers," often housed in temporary quarters or industrial warehouses. Worshipers dress casually, even dressing down from their weekday norm of shirt and tie or even business casual. The ambience of the worship service is informal, as is the music. The sanctified tones of the organ have been replaced by the familiar beat of a rock band. The songs we sing emphasize God's love, grace, and mercy—but less often his sovereignty, holiness, and splendor. We celebrate God with loud singing and raised hands, but not with silence and bowed heads. We come with open arms to be loved by God, but not with bent knees to offer ourselves to him in humble submission.

As you read that last paragraph, you may have wanted to respond, "That's not true! In my church we often worship God in his majesty and offer ourselves to him in humble worship." Great! Many churches haven't lost the importance and meaning of reverent submission. If you worship in such a church, praise God!

But you may also want to present a different objection: "All of that reverent stuff didn't work. Churches with organs, hymns, and pews populated by well-dressed congregants are dying. They're all about form and tradition and outward appearance, not about the condition of the worshipers' hearts. Dynamic churches celebrate God's love and grace. We know God accepts us just as we are—dressed up or not." That's true, and it's a reason for thanksgiving. I've experienced some of the most glorious, celebrative, and reverent worship of my life while wearing shorts and a polo shirt, sitting on a folding chair in a fixed-up warehouse, and being led by a praise band. In fact, in chapter 4 of this book, I urged you to use your body more fully in worship, including gestures often associated with informal, "contemporary" worship.

To be sure, reticence about reverence can take many forms. It can infect traditional churches as well as new, start-up congregations. And there are churches full of casually dressed, rock-band-led worshipers who worship God both reverently and submissively. But I still think my general concern for the loss of reverence in Christian worship remains valid. Just as traditional worship easily became imbalanced and strayed away from the posture of the heart to an emphasis on outward form, so it is with much contemporary worship. With an informal approach to worship and an emphasis on spontaneity, we can lose the sense that we are in the presence of the sovereign, awe-inspiring God of the universe.[3] We need to rediscover the biblical balance, the fullness of prayer and worship. We need both celebration and silence, both exuberant praise and reverent submission.

And, may I add, *you* need these diverse expressions of prayer. My concern isn't just for the church at large, but for your personal relationship with God. Of course, these two are integrally related because your experience of God is profoundly shaped by the worship practices of your church. Consider your practices in both public worship and private devotions. Have you found an appropriate balance between the diverse modes of prayer discussed in this book? Do you revere God even as you seek his grace? Do you submit to him even as you tell him what you'd like him to do for you? Do your prayers reflect the kind of balance we find in Scripture?

The Psalms will help you find and maintain this biblical balance. And as the Psalms prepare us for a balanced life of prayer, they also teach us something about worship that you might find surprising. In scriptural perspective, reverent submission to God isn't just one aspect of worship that needs to be held in balance with the others. Rather, it's the core, the essence, the heart of worship. Without reverence, there is no worship.

The Heart of Worship

Though it sounds almost like heresy to say so, the heart of worship has nothing to do with my feelings or experiences. True worship is not about me, but about the God who has revealed himself in Jesus Christ. And though worship includes both celebration and adoration, it is centered in reverent submission.

Psalm 96 begins with a call to worship that would be at home in almost any praise-based service today:

> O sing to the LORD a new song;
>   sing to the LORD, all the earth.
> Sing to the LORD, bless his name;
>   tell of his salvation from day to day. (verses 1-2)

Then the psalm proclaims God's all-surpassing greatness: "For great is the LORD, and greatly to be praised; he is to be revered above all gods" (verse 4).

Literally, God is "to be *feared* above all gods." This doesn't mean we should hide from God as if he were some hideous monster. But it does mean that God deserves our full, utter respect. Even as we draw near to God in response to his gracious invitation, we remember that our God is a consuming fire, not a glowing candle.[4] The greatness of God demands not just our praise but also our reverence.

Psalm 96 continues:

Ascribe to the LORD, O families of the peoples,
    ascribe to the LORD glory and strength.
Ascribe to the LORD the glory due his name;
    bring an offering, and come into his courts.
Worship the LORD in holy splendor;
    tremble before him, all the earth. (verses 7-9)

The original language speaks of "giving" glory and strength to the Lord, but since we can't do anything to add to God's glory or strength, the translators rightly call us to "ascribe" such things to the Lord. We use our words to celebrate God's excellence. This idea is captured by the original sense of the English word *worship,* which meant "to offer worth to" someone or "to praise a person's value." Thus, in English, when we worship God we offer worth to God by acknowledging God's own incomparable worthiness.

But the biblical verb *worship* suggests an even greater and costlier personal offering than mere words can deliver. In Hebrew, this verb means "to bow down before someone," often with your face to the ground.[5] For example, when Joseph's brothers came to Egypt, they "*worshiped* before him, noses to the ground" (Genesis 42:6, author's translation). The language of bowing before God abounds as well in Psalm 95:

O come, let us worship and bow down,
    let us kneel before the LORD, our Maker!
For he is our God,
    and we are the people of his pasture,
    and the sheep of his hand. (verses 6-7)

The Hebrew verb for "worship" paints a vivid picture of people falling down in reverent submission before God. I add the adjective *reverent* to the noun *submission* because it's possible for submission to be coerced. If a tyrant forces a conquered people to submit, they will do so to avoid losing their lives. But their submission is not worship in the biblical sense because it lacks profound respect and devotion. Reverent submission involves the offering of ourselves to God because we hold him in highest regard and wish to give our lives to him. It's a response to the self-revelation of God and the glory of his self-giving love. Whether we bow down before God physically isn't the main point. True worship involves submitting our whole selves to God, with reverence and devotion. As Matthew Henry observed, "We cannot worship God acceptably, unless we worship him with reverence and godly fear."[6]

Contemporary songwriter Matt Redman has perfectly captured the biblical core of worship in a song he wrote with his wife, Beth. Note the stunning lyrics of "Facedown":

Welcomed in to the courts of the King
I've been ushered in to Your presence
Lord, I stand on Your merciful ground
Yet with every step tread with reverence

And I'll fall facedown
As Your glory shines around
Yes I'll fall facedown
As Your glory shines around.

Who is there in the heavens like You?
And upon the earth, who's Your equal?
You are far above, You're the highest of heights
We are bowing down to exalt You.[7]

Consider your own relationship with God. Do you intentionally offer yourself in submission to God? Do you do this on a regular basis? Do you ever actually kneel before God or bow with your face to the ground? If not, why not? I don't mean to dwell upon the physical posture of prayer, except for the fact that our bodies and our hearts are created to be an integrated unit. Though it's possible to be fully submitted to God without kneeling, in fact, our physical posture can lead our hearts into the heart of worship—the full offering of ourselves to God.

I discovered this truth while serving on the staff of Hollywood Presbyterian Church under Pastor Lloyd Ogilvie. During one of our staff meetings, Lloyd led us in a time of extended prayer. At one point he asked us all to kneel before the Lord. It felt strange to assume a posture of prayer that was so foreign to me. Yet it also felt astoundingly right, as if this was exactly how I should have been praying for decades. While I was on my knees, my heart was drawn into deeper submission to God.

THE IRRESOLVABLE TENSIONS OF PRAYER

Throughout this book we have examined different modes of prayer. At times in your reading you may have felt a nagging tension. Indeed, I've often felt this tension while writing. For example, in one chapter I advocate the open, bold prayer of asking. Yet in another I speak of the need for trustful silence. The chapter on silence appears immediately before a chapter that calls for riotous, joyful shouting to God. And now I'm urging you to approach God in reverent humility, bowing before the King, whereas not long ago I was encouraging you to cozy up into God's lap. Am I hopelessly confused?

I could pass the buck by pointing out that these extreme swings in talking about prayer are not my fault. I could simply blame the Psalms. Here we confront a diversity in prayer that is unexpected, even baffling. As I mentioned earlier, John Calvin's title for the Psalms was "An Anatomy of all the Parts of the Soul."[8] From these Spirit-inspired poems we learn to pour out *everything* in our hearts as we pray.

I'm convinced that the tensions we feel in the Psalms should not be resolved. Though we may want to tidy everything up so we can know exactly how much to submit to God and how much to ask from him, how much to shout for joy and how much to keep silent before him, the Psalms resist such neat and tidy prescriptions. In fact, a *delightful messiness pervades the entire Psalter.*

Consider, for example, the tension between approaching God boldly and humbly. It's hard to imagine how we can come to God on our knees while at the same time saying, "Rouse yourself! Why do you sleep, O Lord? Awake, do not cast us off forever!" (Psalm 44:23). Of course, we can't engage in all expressions of prayer at the same time. But it isn't necessary or even helpful to keep our expressions in neat, separate, and unpsalmlike boxes either.

Look again at Psalm 95. This psalm calls for humble submission: "O come, let us worship and bow down, let us kneel before the LORD, our Maker!" (verse 6). Given what I've said about the meaning of bowing, we'd expect the rationale for our worship to be God's royal sovereignty. His greatness as King is mentioned three verses earlier (verse 3). But the stated reason here for our bowing is not God's kingly authority over us, but his pastoral care for us:

> O come, let us worship and bow down,
>> let us kneel before the LORD, our Maker!
> For he is our God,
>> and we are the people of his pasture,
>> and the sheep of his hand. (verses 6-7)

In this case, the psalmist calls us to respond to God's tender care by bowing reverently before him. The Great King is also the Good Shepherd. Thus, submission flows into devotion, and vice versa. Humble reverence overlaps with thankful comfort. Our relationship with a multifaceted God is also multifaceted, and the separate facets overlap and intertwine.

It's terribly easy for Christians to get into a prayer rut in which we approach God in more or less the same way every time. I remember a young man in my college ministry who always began his prayers by confessing his inadequacy. Of course he was right to confess his sin. But if I called for prayers of praise, he'd begin with, "Lord, I'm so sinful that, apart from your grace, I'd be unable to praise you. Please forgive me for how rarely I offer praise to you." There's nothing wrong with this prayer, but by the fiftieth time, you got the idea that this young man was stuck. Not only did he need a deeper experience of forgiveness, he needed to start praying the Psalms. The diversity of these biblical prayers would have freed him from his prayer rut.

Reverent Submission and Bold Admission

One of the tensions of the Psalms—indeed, of the Bible—is the tension between reverent submission and bold admission. Is God the Great King before whom we bow in utter submission? Or is God the Master of Mercy to whom we can freely bring every need, every anger, every doubt?

The answer, of course, is both/and. God is both Great King and Master of Mercy. Therefore we come before God with reverent submission *and* with bold admission. We come knowing that through Christ we will be admitted into God's presence and that in his presence we can admit everything about our lives—the good, the bad, and the ugly.

Some Christians are inclined to resolve the tension between submission and admission in favor of the latter. After all, isn't God a loving Father who forgives and embraces us? And, as we saw earlier, doesn't the book of Hebrews invite us to come before God with boldness?

Indeed, Hebrews does offer a startling invitation: "Let us therefore approach the throne of grace with boldness, so that we may receive mercy and find grace to help in time of need" (4:16). Yet Hebrews never surrenders God's majesty or awesomeness. Notice that we approach God's *throne,* not his welcome mat. No matter how bold we may be in Christ, we're still coming into the presence of a King who is always worthy of our utter respect.

Later, Hebrews enlarges the picture of the God that we approach through Christ:

> But you have come to Mount Zion and to the city of the living God, the heavenly Jerusalem, and to innumerable angels in festal gathering, and to the assembly of the firstborn who are enrolled in heaven, and to God the judge of all, and to the spirits of the righteous made perfect, and to Jesus, the mediator of a new covenant, and to the sprinkled blood that speaks a better word than the blood of Abel. (12:22-24)

The passage goes on to remind us that God's voice shook the earth when he spoke from Mount Sinai (see verses 25-27). And the implications for us?

> Therefore, since we are receiving a kingdom that cannot be shaken, let us give thanks, by which we offer to God an acceptable worship with reverence and awe; for indeed our God is a consuming fire. (verses 28-29)

There is no logical contradiction between approaching God's throne boldly and offering worship with reverence and awe. God's diverse nature calls forth diverse responses. Our God deserves both intimacy and reverence, both boldness and humility, rather like a beloved school principal.

A Matter of Principals

Agnes Barnes was the principal of my elementary school, and she played this role brilliantly, like Charlton Heston as Moses. One of the first things I learned about Mrs. Barnes from my mother was that she had once spanked one of my relatives with a ruler when he was a student at Glenoaks Elementary School. That made a profound impression on me. I knew that Mrs. Barnes had the power to spank me if she chose to do so. She was, therefore, someone to be feared.

When I first saw Mrs. Barnes in the flesh, I thought she bore an uncanny resemblance to the Old Maid picture in my card game—yet another reason to fear this educational dictator. I examined her carefully for evidence of the dreaded ruler, but to no avail. I figured it must have been hidden in her office, along with other implements of torture. In point of fact, during my six years under her rule, I never heard of any student receiving physical punishment from Mrs. Barnes. Of course, how could I be sure? Maybe the spanked students just disappeared mysteriously, never to be heard from again.

I never saw Mrs. Barnes treat a student with anything other than respect, even when she was rebuking us. She never raised her voice or put anybody down. She didn't have to. She demanded respect by the way she carried herself, by her quiet authority and regal aplomb. If Mrs. Barnes happened to visit a classroom, a wave of silence would magically precede her. Even the notoriously naughty students knew how to act around Mrs. Barnes.

During my first years at Glenoaks Elementary, I avoided Mrs. Barnes when I could. But when I was in sixth grade, the grammar schools in Glendale, California, sponsored a patriotic speech contest. I dutifully entered my speech and, lo and behold, won the contest for my school. For the next couple of months, I delivered my speech to school assemblies and service clubs throughout the city. Who do you think was my escort and companion for these events? That's right, none other than Mrs. Barnes. I spent many hours alone with her, riding in her car and eating lunch with her at civic meetings. She turned out to be a great encourager, the first person outside my family to talk with me about the possibilities for my long-term future. She was the first to suggest that I consider an Ivy League education. She told me I had a bright future in giving speeches. I appreciated Mrs. Barnes and actually enjoyed her company.

But that's not to say I became cozy with her. When the luncheon at the Soroptimist Club included an ample serving of cooked beets, I found myself in a quandary. I hated beets. When my parents made me eat just a single bite of that vile vegetable, I usually gagged and struggled to avoid disgorging the contents of my stomach. But sitting next to Mrs. Barnes, my principal with the mythical ruler, I couldn't simply leave the beets on my plate, and vomiting wasn't a good plan either. So I ate my beets without complaining. My reverence for Mrs. Barnes was that profound.

By the time I graduated from elementary school, I wasn't afraid of Mrs. Barnes any longer. But I didn't ever feel very free with her. I couldn't imagine approaching her with a problem or actually seeking to be with her. On the spectrum that runs from reverence to intimacy, I was way over on the side of reverence.

Now that I am a father of elementary-school children, I have watched with interest their relationship with their principal. My daughter, Kara, has the utmost respect for her principal, Mrs. Parham. If Mrs. Parham were ever to scold Kara, my daughter would probably burst into tears. Without a doubt, this strong principal is in charge of the school and commands respect. But she also receives the kids' love.

A couple of months ago, the school sponsored a fund-raising raffle. Students could purchase tickets and put them in about twenty different boxes. Each box represented a certain prize, including gift certificates, movie coupons, tickets to amusement parks, and candy. It was a child's dream. One of the prizes was lunch with Mrs. Parham. Now if lunch with Mrs. Barnes had been a prize when I was in school, I'm afraid her box might have remained empty (especially if we knew that lunch might include beets). But not so with Mrs. Parham's box. Lots of children wanted to dine with her. Kara took her stack of one hundred tickets, walked past all the other alluring boxes with their glitzy prizes, and put her whole stack in Mrs. Parham's box. More than toys, games, or sweets, Kara wanted to have lunch with her principal. And, wouldn't you know it, she won the drawing! Kara was beside herself with glee.

What explains the fact that Kara wants a relationship with her principal? It's not because Mrs. Parham has lowered the respect bar or that she has become mere buddies with her students. She is still the revered principal, just as Mrs. Barnes was. But unlike Mrs. Barnes, Mrs. Parham readily communicates her affection for her students. She greets them by name, encourages them enthusiastically, and expresses genuine love for them. In return she receives both ample respect and ample love.

Some Christians relate to God as if he were a cosmic Barney, a nauseatingly sweet, big ol' pal who hugs us and loves us and ends up boring us silly. Others of us relate to God as if he were Mrs. Barnes on a really bad day. God gets our distant reverence but nothing more intimate. Scripture teaches us that neither approach is adequate. Rather, we come to God like my daughter comes to Mrs. Parham, with honor and respect, and also with adoration and delight. Our hearts yearn to be with the holy, awesome God who loves us and welcomes us into his presence.

Hebrews gets it right, just like the Psalms. Our God is a consuming fire worthy of reverent worship. And he is also the One who has taken our sin upon himself in Jesus Christ so that we might enjoy an intimate, open relationship with him. Therefore, we can approach God boldly, with no holds barred.

LIVING PRAYERFULLY, LIVING WORSHIPFULLY

If you were to continuing reading beyond Hebrews 12:28-29, you might be surprised. Let me supply this text once again but add the verses that immediately follow:

Therefore, since we are receiving a kingdom that cannot be shaken, let us give thanks, by which we offer to God an acceptable worship with reverence and awe; for indeed our God is a consuming fire. Let mutual love continue. Do not neglect to show hospitality to strangers, for by doing that some have entertained angels without knowing it. (12:28–13:2)

Our English Bibles separate "consuming fire" from "let mutual love," usually by adding both a chapter and a paragraph break. The original Greek manuscripts did not make such a stark division. In the mind of the author of Hebrews, offering acceptable worship with reverence and awe flows naturally into mutual love and hospitality. We worship not only by giving thanks to God but by living worshipfully in the world through serving one another.

When we worship God, we bow humbly before him. We offer ourselves in reverent submission. But this is just the beginning of worship. When a subject comes into the presence of the King and bows down, this is preparation for what follows. The King will issue his command and the subject will go out and implement it. Literal worship leads to literal obedience.

So it is in our relationship with God. Worship isn't limited to what we do in church or in our personal quiet time. It's also a matter of how we live for God in the world. Throughout the Psalms God is the Lawgiver who tells us how to live, the Judge whose justice impels us to live rightly, and the Revealer who speaks his Word so that we might believe and do it.[9] Thus, when we submit ourselves to God in worship we are pledging to do his will in the world, to obey his Word each day.

The work of Christ doesn't nullify the calling to worship God in daily living; it refocuses and intensifies it. To the Romans the apostle Paul wrote, "I appeal to you therefore, brothers and sisters, by the mercies of God, to present your bodies as a living sacrifice, holy and acceptable to God, which is your spiritual worship" (12:1). The underlying Greek speaks not of "spiritual" worship so much as "logical" or "sensible" worship. It's as if Paul were saying, "Here's the worship that really makes sense: to present your bodies as a living sacrifice." And how do we make this presentation? Through the way we live in the world each day, especially as members of Christ's body.

Both Hebrews 12–13 and Romans 12 associate worship with life in the church. Worship is not something we do alone, but in community with other believers. This New Testament emphasis on community is nothing new. It simply reasserts what is true throughout the Old Testament, especially in the Psalms. Psalms 95 and 96 call to worship not the solitary believer but the *community* of believers. Together we sing a new song to the Lord. Together we bow reverently before God. Together we live worshipfully in the world. Moreover, as Psalm 96 makes clear, we live worshipfully in the world so that the world may join us in genuine worship.

Everything I've said in this chapter can enrich your private relationship with God. If you reverently submit yourself to God, you'll discover a new depth of intimacy with him and a new power to live for him. But the Psalms remind us that life with God is something to be shared with others. Kneeling in Lloyd Ogilvie's office for prayer allowed me to offer myself more fully to the Lord. It's an experience I continue to treasure. But this experience was so much richer because it was shared. I wasn't kneeling by myself, but together with several brothers and sisters. In that room were highly regarded leaders not only in the Hollywood church but in the wider Christian church. Yet we were on our knees together, offering our lives to God, seeking his will so that we might obey it together. My colleagues' humility encouraged me, and our shared worship enriched our fellowship together.

As you come to the end of this book, I pray that it has stretched and deepened your personal relationship with God. But I hope as well that you've been able to share this growth with others. If so, keep it up! If not, then why not ask God to show you some people with whom you can share what you've learned? Perhaps you could read this book with your small group, or with a prayer partner, or with your spouse or children.

One of God's greatest gifts to us is intimate fellowship with him. What a privilege to know God, to receive his Word, and to have the freedom to share all that we are with him—no holds barred. But the gift of intimate fellowship with God isn't given in a vacuum, as if the ideal Christian life were one of endless solitude. In fact, as we grow more deeply in relationship with God, he will help us grow more deeply in relationship with his people.[10] We will be like

David and the other psalmists, who penned their psalms so that others might join them in their intimate experiences with God. The psalmists knew that even the most deeply personal encounters with God would become richer when shared with God's people.

If this book helps you pray more fully, I'm glad. If this book helps you know God more intimately and completely, I'm delighted. And if this book helps you live prayerfully each day, presenting your body in worship to God each moment, then what can I do but offer praise to God? The final chapter of the Psalms says it best:

> Praise the LORD!
> Praise God in his sanctuary;
>> praise him in his mighty firmament!
> Praise him for his mighty deeds;
>> praise him according to his surpassing greatness!
> Praise him with trumpet sound;
>> praise him with lute and harp!
> Praise him with tambourine and dance
>> praise him with strings and pipe!
> Praise him with clanging cymbals;
>> praise him with loud clashing cymbals!
> Let everything that breathes praise the LORD!
> Praise the LORD! (150:1-6)

Et cetera, et cetera. Amen!

An Exercise in Prayer of Worship

Pray through Psalm 95 and 96. Allow the words and phrases, the metaphors and images to sink into your soul. Then, if you are able, kneel before God as you read these psalms. (If you can't kneel because of physical limitations, at least you might bow your head.) Don't rush your reading. See if the act of kneeling changes the way you pray. Then try bowing fully before God with your face to the ground. You might pray in this way: "Here I am, Lord. All that I am, I offer to you. I submit myself to you completely. I want to live each day worshiping you." Use your own words to offer yourself to the Lord. Let this be a time of submission and dedication.

QUESTIONS FOR REFLECTION AND GROWTH

Praying with No Holds Barred

T his discussion guide is designed for a variety of uses: personal reflection, discussion with a prayer partner, small-group study, or Christian education in a local church setting. The questions for each chapter vary in their focus. Some relate directly to the content of the chapter. Others are more wide ranging. Many of the questions are meant to help you relate the material of the chapter to your own life in a practical way.

For further study, you may wish to examine more closely the Scripture passages that are highlighted in each chapter.

Introduction: No Holds Barred

1. When, if ever, have you found yourself feeling spiritually dry and parched? Did anything happen to refresh you? If so, what?

2. Have you ever felt yourself holding back in your communication with God? Did a part of you want to say something to God, while another part of you held back? What was going on in your life at that time? Why did you hold back?

3. Have you ever experienced prayer that felt like you were wrestling with God? What happened as a result of your no-holds-barred prayer?

4. In the past, how have you dealt with the "messy" psalms, the ones that express serious doubt, desperation, or vengeance? Do you most often

choose to overlook them? Why? What thoughts and feelings do these psalms express that you wish you could express in your own prayers?

5. Have you ever read through the Psalms on a regular basis? If so, how did this experience affect you?

6. Are you willing to read systematically through the Psalms as a central feature of your devotional life, at least for the next 150 days?

Chapter 1: Hey, God—Get Up!

1. How do you feel about asking for things? In everyday life, are you comfortable with asking questions, asking for help, asking for directions, and so forth? Or are you reluctant to ask for things you need? Explain.

2. When, if ever, are your prayers childlike? Do you feel free to call out to God without being careful to get all the words just right? Why or why not?

3. How do you feel about asking God more than once for the same thing? Have you ever heard Christian teaching that counseled against repeated asking or that encouraged it? What do you believe about this?

4. Before answering this question, give it some thought: Do you pray boldly? Do your prayers convey the rawness and honesty you see reflected in the Psalms? Do you really approach God's throne of grace with boldness? If you do pray boldly, what has helped you do this? And if not, what do you think is holding you back?

5. What do you think of the idea that prayers of asking are meant not only to get answers but also to draw each of us into closer relationship with God? Does the prayer of asking do more for you or for God? Explain.

6. Is there something you've considered asking God for but have hesitated to do so? What, if anything, is stopping you from praying boldly right this moment?

Chapter 2: Praying Like Elephants

1. The Psalms call us to remember what God has done. What difference might it make if you were to recount regularly what God has done in your life?

2. Why do we often forget the things God has done for us? How might prayer of remembering help us avoid taking God and his blessings for granted?

3. Think back to a watershed moment in your life, a time when God touched you in such a way that your life was never the same afterward? What happened in that moment, and what was the result?

4. Do you tend to remember the good times in life more than the bad, or vice versa? How do you think this impacts your relationship with God?

5. How might prayers of remembrance impact not only your own faith but that of your family, your church, your small group, or your prayer partner(s)?

6. We live in a society that values the present to the exclusion of the past. What should we do, as Christians, to help one another think back to what God has done in the past?

Chapter 3: The Quiet After the Storm

1. What makes your life "noisy"? These things could be loud in a physical sense or perhaps just in a spiritual sense. What distracts you from hearing the voice of God?

2. How do you feel about silence? Do you avoid it whenever possible, or do you seek more times of silence?

3. What do you do if you have time alone? Do you find ways to quiet the noise around you, or do you continue to fill your life with noise (television, radio, computer, cell phone, etc.)? Why do you do what you do?

4. When, if ever, have you had an experience of being quieted by God? What happened?

5. What do you think about the idea of a silent retreat? Does this sound appealing? unnecessary? difficult? impossible?

6. What quiets your soul? What helps you be quiet inside?

7. When, if ever, have you had an experience of "hearing God's voice" in a time of quiet? What happened?

Chapter 4: A Standing Ovation for God

1. Were your formative experiences of worship ones that emphasized silence or loud celebration or both? How do you feel about engaging your entire body in prayer and praise to God?

2. What physical expressions, if any, do some people use in worship that you'd rather not experience? What makes you uncomfortable with those forms of worship and praise?

3. What physical expressions are welcome during worship at your church? Why do you think your church is open to these expressions?

4. What physical expressions are *not* welcome in your church? Why not?

5. When in your life have you felt more freedom to be physically expressive in worship? What happened to give you this greater freedom?

6. When, if ever, have you found that your body leads your heart in worship—that physical movement in worship softens your heart toward God? Or is it always the other way around for you? Explain.

7. What might help you offer all that you are to God in worship?

Chapter 5: Groaning in the Night

1. Can you remember a time when you were so distraught that you didn't have words left to pray? If so, what led up to that experience? What did you do?

2. Do you ever wake up in the middle of the night, filled with worry or doubt? What do you do in those times?

3. How do you respond to the idea that God invites the full expression of your doubts and desperation in prayer? Do you feel free to groan in prayer when words escape you? Why or why not?

4. Do you ever doubt God's presence, his goodness, or even that he exists? What do you do in those times? Do you feel free to pray about your doubt? Why or why not?

5. Why do you think we're tempted to hide our doubts from God? Are we trying to avoid hurting God's feelings, or do we not want to fully admit our doubts, even to ourselves?

6. If you really believed, to the depth of your soul, that nothing in all creation could separate you from God's love in Jesus Christ (see Romans

8:35-39), what difference would this make in your relationship with God? Would you then feel free to fully express your bouts of desperation to God? Explain.

Chapter 6: Speaking the Unspeakable

1. Knowing Jesus's teaching to love our enemies and to turn the other cheek, we find it hard to know what to do with the prayers for vengeance that we see in the Psalms. What did you think about those passages before you read chapter 6 on the Psalms' "scandalous imprecations"?

2. Do you think it is acceptable for a Christian to pray as the psalmists did, asking God for revenge? Why or why not?

3. The psalms of vengeance help us pray more fully and authentically in the following ways: (1) We learn to be more honest with God; (2) We pray in solidarity with victims of injustice; (3) We pray against God's enemies; (4) We surrender our vengeful desires; (5) We open our hearts more fully to God's transforming power; (6) We experience once again the grace of the Cross. Which of these points resonates the most with you? Why?

4. What, if anything, did you learn from reading chapter 6 that you had not understood before?

5. In this chapter I tell about a time when I prayed a prayer of vengeance. Have you ever done this? Why or why not? If you did, what was the result of your prayer(s)?

6. Some might say, "Jesus forgave those who crucified him. He called us to forgive as well. Therefore it is never appropriate for us to pray prayers of vengeance. In the New Testament era, such prayers should be avoided." How would you respond to this objection?

Chapter 7: Savoring Life

1. Thanksgiving isn't just a holiday in November. It's a biblical way of life. Would you describe yourself as a thankful person? Would those who know you well agree with that characterization? Explain.

2. If you often forget to be grateful, what keeps you from feeling and expressing gratitude to God? to people?

3. What is most effective in helping you feel and express gratitude?

4. In chapter 7 of this book, I argued that gratitude helps us enjoy life more. Do you agree? Why or why not? Have you ever experienced this dynamic? If so, how did gratitude help you savor life?

5. In this chapter a clear connection is drawn between celebrating Communion (the Eucharist) and expressing thanks. When, if ever, have you experienced the connection between the two?

6. Do you ever get together with other Christians to share in giving thanks to God? If so, what happens inside you when you do this? If you haven't done this, what is holding you back?

Chapter 8: Flooding God

1. In this chapter the point is made that prayer and praise are closely linked. Do most of your prayers include words of praise to God? Why or why not? If not, would you be willing to make this practice a regular habit?

2. In human relationships, do you tend to be generous with praise toward others? Why or why not?

3. How do you feel about *receiving* praise? Is this comfortable for you, or does it make you feel uncomfortable? Explain.

4. What are the benefits of "flooding God" with redundant praise? How can we keep from becoming bored with repetitive praise of God?

5. When in your life have you praised the Lord with great exuberance? What happened as you did this?

6. What difference would it make in your life if you really believed that you were created to "live for the praise of [God's] glory" (Ephesians 1:12)?

Chapter 9: The Dreaded Encounter

1. In this chapter I described a time when, as a teenager, I had to tell my father I had gotten a speeding ticket. Describe a time, if any, when you had to tell someone about a personal mistake or a failing on your part. Did you put off telling the person? What happened when you finally confessed?

2. God already knows everything we've done, said, and thought. So why are we hesitant to confess our sins to God?

3. In general, are you reluctant to talk to God about your sins? If so, what is holding you back?

4. Are there certain sins you have a very hard time admitting to the Lord? What might help you confess even these sins?

5. As you think about your relationship with God, what helps you fully confess your sins to him?

6. Have you ever experienced the joy that comes from knowing God has forgiven you? Have there been special times in your life when the realization of this truth has been especially powerful for you? Explain.

Chapter 10: Facedown Before the King

1. Have you ever physically bowed down before a human being? If so, in what context? How did you feel?

2. Consider the style of worship at your church. Is there more emphasis on casual intimacy with God or on reverence before him? Or is there a fairly even balance? Explain.

3. Have you ever bowed facedown before God? If so, what did you experience as you showed that degree of reverence before the Lord?

4. If you've never bowed before God with your face to the ground, would you be willing to do so? Why or why not?

5. This chapter refers to the "delightful messiness" of the Psalms, meaning that they call for us to pray with noisy celebration and with silence; to pray by asking and also by listening; to pray in worship and praise but also in doubt, desperation, and vengeance. Do you find this messiness "delightful"? Why or why not?

6. Worship involves prayer, and prayer involves worship. How can you live in an attitude of worship toward God, not only in settings of corporate worship, but also in your heart throughout each day?

NOTES

Introduction

1. Friedrich Nietzsche, "The Antichrist," no. 48, quoted in Walter Kaufmann, trans. and ed., *The Portable Nietzsche* (New York: Viking Penguin, 1968), 628.

2. Colin Brown, ed., *The New International Dictionary of New Testament Theology*, vol. 2 (Grand Rapids: Zondervan/Regency, 1976), s.v. *parrhēsia*.

3. Dietrich Bonhoeffer, *Psalms: The Prayer Book of the Bible*, trans. James H. Burtness (Minneapolis: Augsburg, 1970).

4. John Calvin, *Commentary on the Book of Psalms*, vol. 1, trans. James Anderson (1563, French ed.; repr., Grand Rapids: Baker, 1993), xxxvii.

5. Author's paraphrase from the Hebrew.

6. Bonhoeffer, *Psalms*, 26.

7. Eugene Peterson, *Answering God: The Psalms as Tools for Prayer* (San Francisco: HarperSanFrancisco, 1989), 4.

8. See Psalms 3:7; 4:1; 7:6; 9:19; 10:12; 17:13.

9. Calvin, *Commentary on the Book of Psalms*, xxxvii.

10. Ben Patterson, *Deepening Your Conversation with God: Learning to Love to Pray* (Minneapolis: Bethany, 1999), 18. Added emphasis is Patterson's. Although Ben Patterson does not focus on the Psalms, his book is perhaps closer in spirit to mine than any other book I know. The irony of this is that Ben was my predecessor at Irvine Presbyterian Church, where he was the founding pastor. The prayerfulness of the church Ben passed on to me has been an invaluable gift and no doubt helps explain my own passion for meeting God in prayer.

11. In his book on the Psalter, Dietrich Bonhoeffer noted that "only with daily use does one appropriate this divine prayerbook" (Bonhoeffer, *Psalms*, 25). He's right, of course. But don't take Bonhoeffer's advice legalistically. In your effort to pray through the Psalms on a daily basis, you'll no doubt miss a day or two. When this happens, don't despair. And don't try to catch up by

reading several psalms in one sitting. This isn't a race, and there's no prize for finishing first. In fact, the real prize—a deeper and wider relationship with God—comes through slow, not speedy, reading.

12. You may recognize what I'm suggesting as a version of *lectio divina,* a meditative approach to Bible reading that has become more popular in the last two decades, though it is centuries old. For more information on this practice, see the excellent, brief discussion in Chuck Smith, jr., *Epiphany: Discover the Delight of God's Word* (Colorado Springs: WaterBrook, 2003), 155-66. Buddy Owens encourages a similar approach to biblical meditation in his marvelous book *The Way of a Worshiper: Discover the Secret to Friendship with God* (San Clemente, CA: Maranatha, 2002).

13. See the reference to Calvin's commentary on the Psalms in note 4. Inspirational excerpts from this lengthy commentary are found in John Calvin, *Heart Aflame: Daily Readings from Calvin on the Psalms,* ed. Sinclair Ferguson (Phillipsburg, NJ: Presbyterian & Reformed Publishing, 1999). Don Williams's commentary was originally released as two volumes in the *Communicator's Commentary,* later published in paperback in *Mastering the Old Testament.* This series has been re-released as *The Preacher's Commentary* (Nashville: Nelson, 2004).

14. Peterson, *Answering God,* 12. This book is a helpful introduction to praying the Psalms.

15. Peterson, *Answering God,* 18.

Chapter 1

1. The Hebrew headings in the Psalms, which were added by the ancient Jewish editors, often mention David. Seventy-three of the 150 psalms include the Hebrew label *le Dawid,* which means "of David" or "for David." Scholars are divided on the precise meaning of this ambiguous phrase and whether it necessarily implies authorship by David. It could be more of a dedication to David by another writer. But without question, David was both the author of and the inspiration for many of the psalms that bear his name. In this book I will take psalms headed by *le Dawid* as if they were written by David himself.

2. Several scholars suggest that verse 3 should be translated in the form of an imperative: "Try my heart…visit me…test me." This would mean that Psalm

17 has twenty requests in fifteen verses. See A. A. Anderson, *The Book of Psalms,* vol. 1 (Grand Rapids: Eerdmans, 1972), 148.

3. Apparently, David had not been exposed to any of the oft-recommended formulas for prayer—including some that demand that those who pray hold their requests to the very end, after praising God, thanking him, and confessing their sins. David blew right past the niceties and started requesting things of God right and left.

4. In his commentary on Psalm 17:1, John Calvin urged, "Let us learn, also, that when we present ourselves before God in prayer, it is not to be done with the ornaments of an artificial eloquence, for the finest rhetoric and the best grace which we can have before him consists in pure simplicity." John Calvin, *Commentary on the Book of Psalms,* vol. 1, trans. James Anderson (1563, French ed.; repr., Grand Rapids: Baker, 1993), 236.

5. Calvin, *Commentary on the Book of Psalms,* xxxvii.

6. Eugene Peterson, *Answering God: the Psalms as Tools for Prayer* (San Francisco: HarperSanFrancisco, 1989), 6.

7. In the book of Matthew, the so-called Lord's Prayer consists of seven basic requests, beginning with a request that God's name be held in high regard. The prayer includes supplication for basic needs such as food, forgiveness, and protection (see Matthew 6:9-13).

8. Of course Jesus himself exercised this same freedom as he prayed in the Garden of Gethsemane, repeating his request three times (see Matthew 26:36-46). Furthermore, Jesus underscored the benefits of repetitive prayer in his parable about the widow who kept bothering a judge with her demand for justice until he finally gave in. Jesus told this parable to encourage his disciples "to pray always and not to lose heart" (Luke 18:1). His story underscores the value not only of constant prayer but also of repetitive, relentless supplication.

9. Charles Dickens, *Oliver Twist* (London: Penguin, 2002), 15.

10. The loving Father rushes to embrace us (see Luke 15:11-32). The Son, as High Priest, enables us to approach God's throne with boldness (see Hebrews 4:14-16). The Spirit helps us pray in our weakness (see Romans 8:26-27).

11. See also Psalm 27:4,8-10.

12. See Genesis 1 and 2.

13. For more on this idea, see Ben Patterson's treatment of work and prayer in *The Grand Essentials* (Downers Grove, IL: InterVarsity, 1994).

Chapter 2

1. For more on this idea, see my book *After "I Believe": Experiencing Authentic Christian Living* (Grand Rapids: Baker, 2002).
2. See Luke 22:19; 1 Corinthians 11:24-25.
3. Matt Redman, "When My Heart Runs Dry," copyright © 2001 Thankyou Music. Administered by EMI Christian Music Publishing. Used by permission. All rights reserved.
4. *Avalon,* directed by Barry Levinson (Tri-Star Pictures, 1990). Screenplay based on the book by Barry Levinson, *Avalon, Tin Men, Diner: Three Screenplays* (New York: Atlantic Monthly Press, 1990), see especially pages 243 and 372.

Chapter 3

1. For further discussion of the relationship between quiet and divine guidance, see my book *After "I Believe": Experiencing Authentic Christian Living* (Grand Rapids: Baker, 2002).
2. Question 1 of the *Westminster Shorter Catechism* (Great Britain, 1647). Public domain.
3. John Calvin, *Commentary on the Book of Psalms,* vol. 2, trans. James Anderson (1563, French ed.; repr., Grand Rapids: Baker, 1993), 425.

Chapter 4

1. This is a quotation from Habakkuk 2:20.
2. In Hebrew, the following plural imperatives appear in the Psalms as instructions to do something that communicates to God: bless, praise, sing praise, bow, thank, exult, sing, shout, sing for joy, clap hands, lift hands. I have counted 120 of these imperatives, though there are probably more.
3. For an in-depth discussion of our nature as whole beings, see Dallas Willard, *Renovation of the Heart: Putting on the Character of Christ* (Colorado Springs: NavPress, 2002).

4. Pete Sanchez Jr., "I Exalt Thee," copyright © 1977 Pete Sanchez Jr. Administered by Gabriel Music, Inc., PO Box 840999, Houston, Texas 77284-0999.

5. Frances R. Havergal, "Take My Life and Let It Be," 1874. Public domain.

Chapter 5

1. See 1 Chronicles 6:31-39 and 2 Chronicles 29:30 in which Asaph is called a "seer" and recognized as a writer of praise songs.

2. Francis Brown, S. R. Driver, Charles A. Briggs, *A Hebrew and English Lexicon of the Old Testament* (Oxford: Clarendon, 1979), s.v. *hamah.*

3. See Psalm 55:17, in which moaning seems to include words, though not necessarily.

4. Matthew Henry, *Matthew Henry's Concise Commentary of the Bible* (Grand Rapids: Christian Classics Ethereal Library, n.d.), Psalm 77, emphasis added; from Gospel Communications, www.gospelcom.net/eword/comments/psalm/mhc/psalm77.

5. See Mark 9:14-29.

6. Biblical injunctions to have faith and not doubt include Matthew 21:21, Mark 11:23, John 20:27, and James 1:6-8.

Chapter 6

1. Dietrich Bonhoeffer, *Psalms: The Prayer Book of the Bible,* trans. James H. Burtness (Minneapolis: Augsburg, 1970), 56.

2. Eugene Peterson, *Answering God: The Psalms as Tools for Prayer* (San Francisco: HarperSanFrancisco, 1989), 98.

3. Peterson, *Answering God,* 98.

4. Peterson, *Answering God,* 98.

5. Peterson, *Answering God,* 100.

6. Walter Brueggemann, *The Message of the Psalms: A Theological Commentary* (Minneapolis: Augsburg, 1984), 87.

7. C. S. Lewis, *Reflections on the Psalms* (1958; repr., San Diego: Harcourt/Harvest, 1986), 33.

8. Bonhoeffer, *Psalms,* 57.

9. Brueggemann, *The Message of the Psalms,* 85. Emphasis in original.

10. See Psalm 22:1 and Mark 15:34; Psalm 31:5 and Luke 23:46.

11. Bonhoeffer, *Psalms,* 59.

Chapter 7

1. See James 1:17: "Every generous act of giving, with every perfect gift, is from above, coming down from the Father of lights, with whom there is no variation or shadow due to change."

2. Francis Brown, S. R. Driver, Charles A. Briggs, *A Hebrew and English Lexicon of the Old Testament* (Oxford: Clarendon Press, 1979), s.v. *yadah.*

3. For another example of thanksgiving in the midst of suffering, see Psalm 69.

4. John Calvin, *The Institutes of the Christian Religion,* trans. Henry Beveridge (Grand Rapids: Eerdmans, 1995), 3.20.28 (compact disk). Spelling of "honour" changed to "honor."

5. Thomas Merton, *Thoughts in Solitude* (Garden City, NY: Image Books, 1968), 43.

6. John Calvin, *Institutes,* 3.20.28. "Favour" changed to "favor."

7. Isaac Watts, "When I Survey the Wondrous Cross," 1707. Public domain.

8. Matt Redman, "Once Again," copyright © 1995 Thankyou Music. Administered by EMI Christian Music Publishing. Used by permission. All rights reserved.

Chapter 8

1. See, for example, Psalm 35:18: "Then I will thank you in the great congregation; in the mighty throng I will praise you."

2. For an example of the reverse, see Psalms 106:1 and 113:9.

3. Quotation from the *Talmud,* Berakoth 4b, quoted in A. J. Rosenberg, *Psalms: A New English Translation,* vol. 3 (New York: Judaica Press, 1991), 535.

4. For example, the verb *sing aloud* appears in Psalm 98:4: "Make a joyful noise to the LORD, all the earth; break forth into *joyous song* and sing praises."

5. Author's paraphrase.

6. John Calvin, *Commentary on the Book of Psalms,* vol. 5, trans. James Anderson (1563, French edition; repr., Grand Rapids: Baker, 1993), 275.

7. See Psalm 96:1, for example.

8. I have addressed in greater depth the issue of seeker-sensitive worship in my article, "Should Worship Be Seeker-Sensitive?" *Worship Leader Magazine,* September/October 2001, 36-40.

9. Question 1 of the *Westminster Shorter Catechism* (Great Britain, 1647). Public domain.

10. Rick Warren, *The Purpose-Driven Life: What on Earth Am I Here For?* (Grand Rapids: Zondervan, 2002), 63.

11. C. S. Lewis, *Reflections on the Psalms* (1958; repr., San Diego: Harcourt/Harvest, 1986), 95.

12. Lewis, *Reflections on the Psalms,* 97.

13. This is the version of Revelation 11:15 and 19:16 that comes from the lyrics of the *Messiah* by George Frideric Handel (1741).

14. English version of the centuries' old liturgical hymn, the "Gloria Patri." Public domain.

Chapter 9

1. See the story of David's sin and repentance in 2 Samuel 11–12.

2. Francis Brown, S. R. Driver, Charles A. Briggs, *A Hebrew and English Lexicon of the Old Testament* (Oxford: Clarendon Press, 1979), s.v. *yadah.*

3. See John 16:7-11.

4. Once again, see Hebrews 4:12-16.

5. The Hebrew verb *bara'* appears in Psalms 51:10, 89:12, 89:47, 102:18, 104:30, and 148:5.

6. John Calvin, *Commentary on the Book of Psalms,* vol. 2, trans. James Anderson (1563, French edition; repr., Grand Rapids: Baker, 1993), 298.

7. Matthew Henry, *Matthew Henry's Concise Commentary of the Bible* (Grand Rapids: Christian Classics Ethereal Library, n.d.), Psalm 32, emphasis added; from Gospel Communications, www.gospelcom.net/eword/comments/psalm/mhc/psalm32.

Chapter 10

1. Richard Rodgers and Oscar Hammerstein II, *The King and I,* directed by Walter Lang (1956). Based on the book by Margaret Landon, *Anna and the King of Siam* (New York: HarperCollins, 1944).

2. *Wayne's World,* directed by Penelope Spheeris (Paramount Pictures, 1992).

3. For a wonderful exception to what I'm saying here, see Matt Redman's contemporary worship album *Facedown,* copyright © 2004 Thankyou Music. Here is a unique and moving combination of rock music that expresses a profound reverence for God's glory and majesty.

4. See Deuteronomy 4:24; Hebrews 12:29.

5. Willem A. VanGemeren, ed., *New International Dictionary of Old Testament Theology and Exegesis* (Grand Rapids: Zondervan, 1997), s.v. *chwh.*

6. Matthew Henry, *Matthew Henry's Concise Commentary on the Bible* (Grand Rapids: Christian Classics Ethereal Library, n.d.), Hebrews 12:18-29; from Gospel Communications, www.gospelcom.net/eword/comments/hebrews/mhc/hebrews12.htm.

7. Matt and Beth Redman, "Facedown," copyright © 2004 Thankyou Music. Administered by EMI Christian Music Publishing. Used by permission. All rights reserved.

8. John Calvin, *Commentary on the Book of Psalms,* vol. 1, trans. James Anderson (1563, French edition; repr., Grand Rapids: Baker, 1993), xxxvii.

9. See, for example, Psalms 19, 99, and 119.

10. I have explored the diverse nature of intimate fellowship with God and his people in my book *After "I Believe": Experiencing Authentic Christian Living* (Grand Rapids: Baker, 2002).

ABOUT THE AUTHOR

MARK D. ROBERTS is a pastor, author, speaker, and blogger. Since 1991 he has been the senior pastor of Irvine Presbyterian Church in Irvine, California. Before coming to Irvine, Mark served as pastor of education on the staff of the First Presbyterian Church of Hollywood, California. He studied at Harvard University, receiving a BA in philosophy, an MA in religion, and a PhD in New Testament and Christian Origins. He teaches classes for several graduate schools, including Fuller Theological Seminary and San Francisco Theological Seminary.

Mark has written several books: *Dare to Be True* (WaterBrook); *Jesus Revealed* (WaterBrook); *After "I Believe"* (Baker); and *Ezra, Nehemiah, Esther* (Word and Nelson). He has also published articles in a number of magazines, including *Leadership* and *Worship Leader,* to which he is a regular contributor. He speaks for churches and other Christian groups and has been interviewed on radio programs nationwide.

Mark's Web site, *www.markdroberts.com,* features his daily blog on matters of Scripture, theology, church, and culture. This site also includes dozens of complimentary resources on a wide variety of topics. These resources have been used by Christians throughout the world for personal study, small-group study, and adult classes.

Mark and his wife, Linda, a marriage and family counselor, have two children and reside in Southern California.

Thought-provoking books
from author Mark D. Roberts

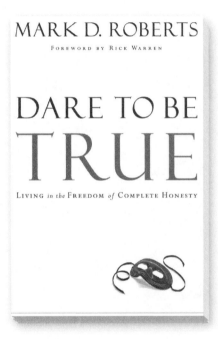

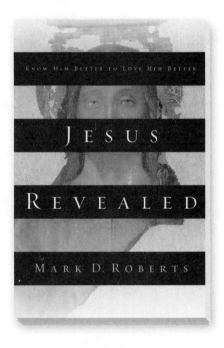

Dare to Be True gives you a bold, direct plan to live the life of truthfulness—the life of ultimate freedom—the life that connects you most intimately with the God of truth.

Jesus Revealed goes beyond the familiar stories and simplified explanations to reintroduce you to the authentic Son of God, so you can love him more fully and follow him more completely.

Available in bookstores and from online retailers

WATERBROOK PRESS
www.waterbrookpress.com